William

A History of Scotland

Book Two

Oxford University Press 1984

Oxford University Press, Walton Street, Oxford OX2 6DP

Oxford London
New York Toronto Melbourne Auckland
Kuala Lumpur Singapore Hong Kong Tokyo
Delhi Bombay Calcutta Madras Karachi
Nairobi Dar es Salaam Cape Town

and associated companies in
Beirut Berlin Ibadan Mexico City Nicosia

Oxford is a trade mark of Oxford University Press
© William Moffat 1984

First published 1984

ISBN 0 19 917043 6

Phototypeset by Tradespools Limited,
Frome, Somerset.
Printed in Hong Kong.

Contents

The Norman Influence **4**

Border Business **18**

The Golden Years **28**

One Nation **34**

The Freedom Fighters **42**

The Hammer and the Lion **48**

A King without a Kingdom **60**

For Freedom Alone **72**

Scotland's Two Kings **78**

The House of the High Steward **90**

The Norman Influence

Castles

In the reign of King Edgar, and even more so while his two brothers Alexander and David held the throne, something new and very important began to happen in Scotland. Common people were troubled by the changes that were afoot, particularly in Galloway and Strathclyde. Great building projects were in progress. Gangs of local peasants were forced to labour long hard hours under the direction of mail clad men, newcomers to the land. Huge circular ditches were dug, deep and wide. The spoil cast up by their spades was heaped high to form a rising mound of earth. From nearby forest land straining teams of oxen dragged the felled timbers to the sites of the new castles. More than two hundred of them rose in Scotland during the 12th century not only in the south, but north beyond the Forth and in Moray. From their wooden gates rode out the grim mailed soldiers of the garrisons to subdue the people and keep the King's peace.

below David I and Malcolm IV in one of the earliest known illustrations of the Kings of Scotland

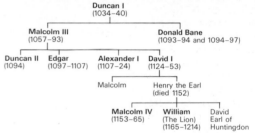

Duncan I (1034–40)

Malcolm III (1057–93) — Donald Bane (1093–94 and 1094–97)

Duncan II (1094), Edgar (1097–1107), Alexander I (1107–24), David I (1124–53)

Malcolm — Henry the Earl (died 1152)

Malcolm IV (1153–65), William (The Lion) (1165–1214), David Earl of Huntingdon

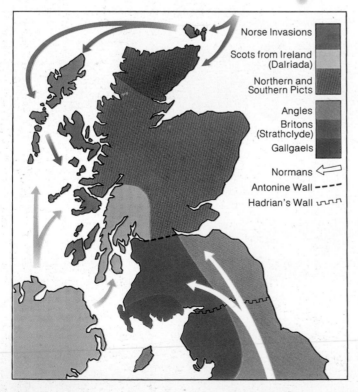

Norse Invasions
Scots from Ireland (Dalriada)
Northern and Southern Picts
Angles
Britons (Strathclyde)
Gallgaels
Normans
Antonine Wall – – – –
Hadrian's Wall

The Normans arrive

A new people had come to Scotland to add to the mix that would make our nation. They had not come as a great army with pennoned lances and gaudy banners, nor as settlers to occupy parts of the land pushing out the local people, but by Royal invitation. They were people of power and wealth come to take important places in Church and State, to help rule the country. They were the Normans.

There was only one king in Scotland but even he called his subjects by their race names; the Scots of Scotia in the north, the English or Angles of the Lothians in the south-east, the Britons of Strathclyde and the Galwegians of Galloway in the south-west. It was one kingdom but certainly not one nation. Now there were the Normans too and they had to be rewarded with lands and power for the services they gave to the Scottish king. In the reign of David I most, if not all, of the valleys of the south were given to Norman families. New names were now heard in Scotland—Agnew, Boswell, Colville, Fraser, Hay, Melville, Menzies, Barclay, Grant and many more. It was a wise and safe policy for a monarch to surround himself with powerful friends who were good soldiers and who would put down unruly rivals while keeping his subjects in order. With these Norman friends of David, and Malcolm IV who succeeded him, came a great wave of change in both state and church.

Protection

In Europe, when the Roman Empire was crumbling and the Roman peace could not be kept, peasants, in fear for their lives, found safety by offering their loyal service to some powerful lord in return for his protection. Small farmers who could not meet the rising land taxes, could escape the impossible burden by giving away their land to a rich landowner who, in return, would allow the farmer to be a tenant for life. Only when he died did the land pass to the landlord.

Over the centuries and in the heat of brutal warfare these two ideas grew. They developed best in France, where constant fighting between districts made the need for protection all the greater. And the best protection was cavalry. The horse had become a major weapon of war.

But horses were expensive. Even rich landlords found it taxing on their wealth to support a large body of soldiers with their horses. A cheaper way was to grant areas of spare land to the men on which they could keep their own horses, whilst remaining in the loyal service of their overlord. From this practice there emerged a new class of men. They were called knights.

As the mound rose squads of men would pack the earth tight and firm until it reached its full height. Next, the circular top was carefully levelled off. Round this great earthen platform was erected a stockade of solid timber with heavy gates to defend the entrance. Up the steep slope to the gateway, logs were set firm in the hard packed soil to make the climb easier. The only way across the deep ditch was a narrow wooden bridge which led straight to these steps.

High on this mound, or motte as it was called, and within the protection of the stockade, the carpenters raised a square tower of timber, strong but still light enough to stand securely on the man-made hill. The ground floor was for stores. It had neither door nor windows—no way in. Steps, which could be removed, led up to the entrance on the first floor where the living quarters were. A square pointed roof covered the tower and the wood was finished in bright colours. It was clear for all to see that attacking such a place would be no easy matter.

A second ditch protected the motte, sometimes all the way round and sometimes joining the first ditch at the narrow bridge and forming a huge figure eight. On the inside bank of the new ditch another stockade was built. Again one narrow bridge leading to a heavy gate spanned the deep wide trench. Any who would force an entry to the tower must first fight their way across two narrow bridges, through at least two heavy gates, up a very steep slope and into a tower with no doorway. The area enclosed by the second ditch and stockade was called the bailey. Within its protection stood chapel, kitchen and outhouses, the stables, barn and byre.

The Feudal System

The system grew till at last everyone became part of it. The King owned all the land. He granted parts of his kingdom to his Barons and Earls, in return for past services and those to come. In turn the Barons and Earls made grants for similar reasons and promises to their knights. Below the knights were the free tenants renting their farms for money or produce from their lord. Lowest of all were the serfs, bound to their place of birth and unable even to marry without the consent of their lord.

This social order came to England with William the Conqueror in 1066. It came to Scotland more than half a century later by Royal invitation. It was called the Feudal System.

In the Lowlands the old Celtic ideas of tribe and kinship were replaced by a new kind of leadership and loyalty. No longer was a man's worth to be measured in the number of cattle he owned. Land was now the measure of rank. But high in their mountains and glens and rocky islands the northern Scots clung to the ancient ways and the clans remained strong.

The feudal system bound the people of this northern kingdom to the service of Norman

Great men knelt bareheaded before their King and, placing their hands in his, promised to love what he loved and to hate what he hated. His friends would be their friends, his enemies their enemies. Lesser men knelt before their superiors to give similar oaths all in the presence of the bible or other holy things. To break such a solemn promise would be a terrible sin. And this was a two way bargain. The overlord was required to keep his word to his man, to protect him and seek justice for him.

overlords and to the land on which they laboured, but it also helped to make living more secure and better organised. It was a hard life for the common folk but it always had been. Now at least there was some protection from warring bands of greedy neighbours.

Towns

The Norman friends of the king brought more than this to Scotland. During the reign of David I not only did a rash of motte and bailey castles spread over the countryside but another kind of building was taking place. Again these were places in which people would live, not a new kind of castle and certainly not villages. A village was simply a group of cottages sharing grazing and crop land. This was something quite different. These were Scotland's first burghs, or towns. They grew up beside a royal castle, or where important roads met or crossed the shallow waters of a river; or in the shadow cast by the walls of some great monastery or church. They were always near the sea or on a river flowing into the sea. And all of these new towns had something in common. They were places of trade. They each had a market. More than that, they were places where raw materials were made into finished goods, for sale.

The Feudal system

The Royal Burghs

King David created more than a dozen burghs on his Royal lands. In the west there were Renfrew and Rutherglen on the south bank of the Clyde. To the north of the Firth of Forth stood Dunfermline, Crail and Inverkeithing, while to the south were Edinburgh and Linlithgow. Stirling was further upstream where the river could be crossed. Old Roxburgh guarded the place where the Teviot flowed into the Tweed and each could be forded, perhaps two miles north-east of the present village. Further east, Berwick overlooked the mouth of the same river where a bridge allowed traders to cross. Haddington on the Tyne was eighteen miles east of Edinburgh. And Perth, once Berr Tatha (meaning 'the height of the Tay') was placed where the river was bridged before it widens to become the Firth of Tay. In the north beyond the Mounth, Elgin, capital of Moray was built where the River Lossie twists and turns before swinging north to flow into the Moray Firth. These were the King's Burghs. Later they would be called Royal Burghs and later there would be more, as many as sixty-six. They were formed at the King's command and by his charter.

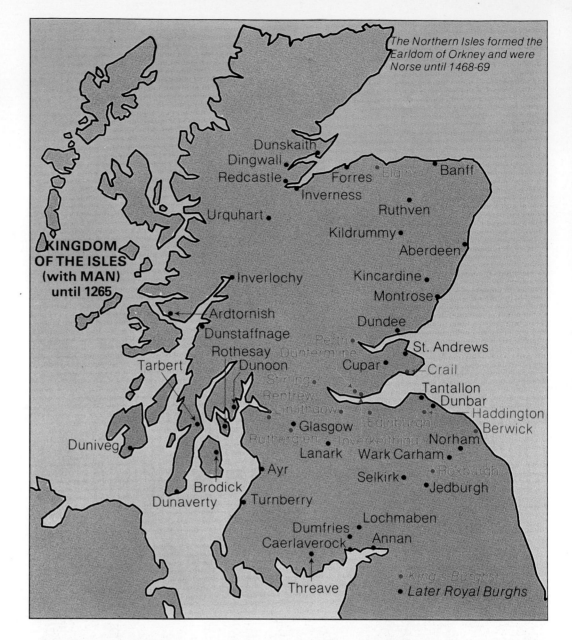

The Northern Isles formed the Earldom of Orkney and were Norse until 1468-69

Dunskaith
Dingwall
Redcastle
Forres
Elgin
Banff
Inverness
Urquhart
Ruthven
Kildrummy
Aberdeen

KINGDOM OF THE ISLES (with MAN) until 1265

Inverlochy
Kincardine
Montrose
Ardtornish
Dundee
Dunstaffnage
Perth
St. Andrews
Rothesay
Dunfermline
Tarbert
Dunoon
Cupar
Crail
Stirling
Tantallon
Renfrew
Dunbar
Linlithgow
Haddington
Duniveg
Glasgow
Edinburgh
Berwick
Rutherglen
Inverkeithing
Norham
Lanark
Wark Carham
Brodick
Ayr
Selkirk
Roxburgh
Dunaverty
Turnberry
Jedburgh
Lochmaben
Dumfries
Caerlaverock
Annan
Threave

• *King's Burghs*
• *Later Royal Burghs*

By the time King David began creating his towns, Scotland had a money system and this was part of the reason that the burgh business began. If groups of people could get together to carry on trade then the King could impose various kinds of tolls and taxes; now that there was silver coinage, these would be paid in money rather than in crops or livestock. So, instead of granting his lands for farming, the King could now use them for raising ready money to pay the royal expenses in peace and war. But it would be very expensive for the King to build new towns, so a better way had to be found. It worked like this. First the King chose a likely spot for a town—perhaps where a market already existed or could be expected to exist—beside a castle or monastery where finished goods would be needed or prepared for sale. Then he issued his charter—a kind of royal special offer! It was meant to attract traders and was advertised through the Church.

Coins of the period

The Charter of Ayr

The oldest surviving charter in Scotland was first proclaimed about the year 1200 by William the Lion and set up the Royal Burgh of Ayr on the west coast. It was all in Latin, of course, but this is what it said –

'William, by the grace of God, King of Scots, to the bishops, abbots, earls, barons, justiciars, sheriffs, provosts, officials and all honest men of his whole land, clerical and lay, greeting. Let those present and to come know that I have made a burgh at my new castle upon Ayr and have granted to the same burgh and to my burgesses dwelling in it all the liberties and all the free customs which my other burghs and my burgesses dwelling in them have throughout my kingdom. I have also allotted in it a market day every Saturday. I have also allowed to the burgesses who shall come thither to inhabit my burgh and settle and dwell there that they be free from toll and from all other custom for their proper goods throughout my whole land. I therefore strictly forbid anyone in my kingdom, on pain of my full forfeiture, to exact from any of them toll or any other custom for their proper goods. Further, I have granted to the same burgh of mine and to my burgesses who shall settle and dwell in that burgh the five pennylands which belong to the town of Ayr.'

The Charter then goes on to describe the exact boundaries of the Five Pennylands which covered an area of about 2,300 acres. After this, came more special offers—

'I have also allowed to my burgesses dwelling there that with each full toft of theirs they may have six acres of land which they have cleared from wood within the foresaid five pennylands, making their own profit therefrom and paying me twelvepence annually for each toft and six acres adjoining it. I therefore command and strictly order that all men who come to that foresaid burgh of mine with their merchandise to sell and buy have my firm peace and use the market and return well and in peace. I also order strictly that toll and other customs which are owed to the burgh be given and received at Mach, Karnebuth, Loudoun, Crosenecon and Lachtalpin. I also strictly forbid anyone, on pain of my full forfeiture, to presume to carry off beyond the foresaid bounds, toll or any other custom which he ought by reason to give to my foresaid burgh.'

The charter finishes by giving a list of the important people who witnessed its issue.

The Town of Ayr

To all those who would begin a new life in his new town on the River Ayr, King William offered—a weekly market at which to sell goods for private profit; freedom from all tolls when travelling about the kingdom on business; a croft of six acres to go along with the building plot, all for the modest yearly rental of twelve pence; the free use of the wide common lands on which to cut wood, peat, heather and to quarry stone; and the King's own peace and safe conduct on travel throughout the dangerous countryside. The King's loyal townsfolk would have good conditions of service and his protection under which to conduct their trade. And so by making it a worthwhile business, the King was able to attract the right kind of loyal people to live in his new towns and enjoy the benefits there. In this way the towns were built and the King could draw income for the royal treasury from the tolls, taxes and rents which he imposed.

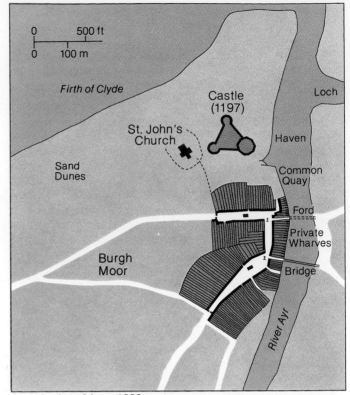

An early plan of Ayr c.1220

In return for all this the burgess had to perform certain duties in the service of his king. Apart from the rent he paid for the land, an oath of loyalty had to be sworn to both the King and the King's burgh. Within a year of being granted his building plot he had to erect his house upon it and dwell there. The plots were slender, only a few metres in width, and so the two storey timber house would have its gable end towards the wide market place and its doorway down the dark narrow lane that led between the buildings to the long strip of back garden. There, at the foot, a strong wooden palisade was to be put up to join with those to either side making a defence all around the new town. This stockade was pierced only where the roads carrying traders to and from the market entered the town. Heavy gates protected these openings. Each burgess was required to hold himself ready to keep watch and, if necessary, take up arms, which he must supply himself, to defend the King's burgh.

Town Plans

They were not big towns like today's, of course. Even the largest would have only a few hundred people living in it and would be little more than a cluster of brightly painted timber houses crowded along both sides of the market place. What streets there were bore names which told exactly where they led. They had no surface paving, only the trodden earth deeply rutted by the wheels of heavy carts. Market street was the main route through the town, the King's Highway and so called the Highgait or High Street. The back lane which wandered behind the houses and close to the palisade was used by the burgesses taking their cattle to and from the pasture lands outside the town. It was called the Cowgait. If there was a Quarrygait, it led to a quarry; a Woodgait to a wood; a Seagait to the sea.

Squalor

Nor were they very trim and tidy, these new burghs. In the streets all kinds of refuse lay in heaps where it fell, to be cleared on to dunghills only once per week. Pigs and poultry had the run of the places and there was no proper sanitation. And always there was the dread of fire which, once kindled, would rage with a terrible swiftness through the huddle of timber and thatch. To guard against this was the duty of all and required by law. No naked flame would be carried between the houses. Tall ladders would be kept from which to fight the roof-top blaze.

The Market and the Fair

But for all their smallness and all their squalor these burghs of the King were busy bustling places, quite unlike anything there had ever been in Scotland. One day in every week the wide market would fill with stalls displaying and selling all kinds of goods—richly coloured cloths of wool and silk; leather goods and metal ware; food and fuel; pots and pottery. In the air the smell of ale and new bread warm from the ovens, mingled with the tang of raw butcher meat and fresh fish. And the stir was even greater at the annual fair when, for a fortnight, the usual rules and laws were relaxed and the market teemed with new-comers—landward men, packmen, merchants from overseas.

Beyond and above the roof tops could be seen the swaying masts of tall merchant ships riding at anchor or by the quayside.

Trade

The King's burgh threw open its gates to the people of farm and village so that they could bring in their fuel and food, wool and skins. The townsfolk would buy these for personal use or to make finished goods for sale. By bringing the country folk together on market day, competition was kept up and prices for the burgesses, kept down. The King's command forbade villagers to sell their produce at any other time or in any other place. They had to take what they could get and be content to pay the King's tolls for the privilege. And at fairs the burghs attracted trade from overseas bringing new goods and greater riches into the country.

Tolls

The King took his share of the new wealth in tolls. There were tolls on just about everything whether coming by land or water, in carts, by pack train even on the walking of cattle or swine. They were collected at town gates, bridges and fords, on the seashore and shire boundaries, in port, anchorage and harbour. And there were market dues to be paid on all goods sold. From these tolls the King filled his treasury with ready money.

These prosperous little towns attracted foreign merchants to Scotland to settle and share in the market, paying their dues and bringing their wealth.

Guilds

The burghs gathered together people who shared an interest in trade rather than tribe. Though the burgesses did not have the great riches or power of the barons they banded together to form strong groups to defend and extend their rights and privileges. They were called 'guilds' and were open to all burgesses whether they made their living buying and selling or as the employers of craftsmen. The guild looked after its members. It supported widows and helped those members

Guildsmen undergoing guild exams to maintain quality standards

who were in business difficulties. The burgh councils were elected from the guild brethren, the law was administered by them and the stubborn defence of the towns was in their hands. The guilds set quality standards and fixed prices for goods sold in the market. They made sure that only members were permitted to trade. Even exporting and importing were under guild control. They worked hard to see that all marketing in their town was carried out in ways that suited them. To lend proper dignity to their courts and meetings the guild members put up a fine building richly furnished and decorated. They were proud to walk in solemn parade to their fine new guildhall, there to make laws, fix prices or judge the wrongdoer. Now the burgesses had their place too, like the baron's castle, like the bishop's church. Men of business now joined men of rank and men of God in the affairs of the kingdom. Within the walls of the burgh was a whole new lifestyle. Now for the first time in Scotland it was possible to prosper without being a farmer. In time they would grow until almost all the people would live in towns.

Abbeys and Monasteries

And there was another kind of building, the grandest yet to be seen in Scotland, now taking place throughout the kingdom—at Dunfermline and Arbroath, at Edinburgh, Dryburgh, Jedburgh and many other places too. Much of the wealth drawn by the King from his burghs was being poured into these great new projects. Master craftsmen in the cutting and carving of wood and stone, metalsmiths and makers of glass too, were brought from England and France. Sites were cleared and workshops erected. Stone was quarried and timber felled. People gathered to watch in wonder as the work progressed.

King David I, the youngest son of the saintly Queen Margaret, began a building of abbeys and monastries such as would never again be known in Scotland. The kingdom was alive with the new spirit and the great work was carried on by the kings that followed—Malcolm IV and his brother William the Lion, Alexander II and Alexander III. Gone were the Celtic men of God with their simple living and ready help for man in his suffering. Now the priests were men set apart from the people by the grand buildings in which they worshipped. Now it was a feudal church with overlords and underlings and only the chosen few would be admitted to its full mystery. The ordinary folk must be content to pray to their God from the other side of a screen made by man.

Years passed before the building reached the height of its eaves. Great timbers were then hoisted on straining ropes by men, perched high on platforms atop the completed walls, heaving on windlass or block and tackle.

From these beams the carpenters assembled huge frames, driving home pegs of hard oak to hold the joints fast under the weight of the massive roof. The slim walls were heavily buttressed against its outwards thrust.

Foundation trenches were dug deep in the clay while all around in the workshops stonecutters shaped the blocks, blacksmiths forged the tools, carpenters prepared stout props and beams to support the construction work. On a concrete bed of mortar and small stones the foundations were laid, block by block, course by course, within the trenches, until ground level was gained. On this solid base rose the lofty walls, built of finely dressed stonework and pierced by tall windows each rising to a graceful arch.

The glassmakers worked at their furnaces to make glass of every colour from which to fashion windows. The glass was cut in pieces to match the plan and joined by strips of lead to form panes. These were braced by iron rods and fixed into the stone mouldings which trimmed and sometimes divided the window spaces.

In the sheds of the master carpenters great doors were fashioned to be hung on the blacksmith's iron hinges and held secure by his iron locks. In the foundries the master metalsmiths cast bells of bronze to be hoisted to the belfry, there to swing and peal out across the countryside.

And high above all soared the slender spire pointing up to the heavens.

Inside the abbey church, the people would seem puny under the lofty arches of the vaulted ceiling, and poor beside the jewelled glitter of gold and silver ornaments, the richness of the drapes and furnishing. They would be kept in their lowly place before a beautiful screen of carved stone which divided the congregation from the most holy parts, shielding from their eyes the Cross. Through this marvellous barrier would come the solemn priests in flowing robes of rich and beautiful cloths to perform the Mass and allow the common folk a brief moment of grace.

For those who had known nothing more than their tiny squat cottages of mud and wattle it was an amazing sight, truly the House of God built and adorned to 'shine like the very fields of Paradise!' They felt properly humble in the presence of such majestic holiness.

15

Worksection

The Norman Influence
Understand Your Work

Castles
1 What great building work troubled the common people?
2 In whose reigns did the new castle building begin?
3 How did the builders make their high mound for the castle?
4 How was the top of the mound enclosed?
5 How was the door to the keep protected?
6 What name was given to the mound?
7 Who guarded the castles?
8 How was it made difficult for anyone to attack the castle?

The Normans
1 How did the Normans enter Scotland without fighting?
2 Was Scotland a single nation in the reign of David I?
3 What new names were now heard in Scotland?
4 Can you find more Norman names?
5 What was the wise thing for King David to do if he was to make himself safe?
6 How did powerful friends help the King?
7 What positions did important Normans occupy in Scotland?
8 What races made up the kingdom of Scotland in the 12th century?

Protection
1 Why did fighting and war break out in Europe?
2 How did European peasants try to find safety?
3 What way was there for small farmers of Europe to escape from their growing debts?
4 How did French landowners meet the cost of keeping a body of cavalry?
5 What were these soldiers on horseback called?
6 How did they repay their overlord?
7 What system grew out of this?

The Feudal System
1 How was the Feudal System arranged from top to bottom?
2 In what way were serfs different from the other ranks?
3 How did people show their intention to be loyal to a superior?
4 Did the superior have to promise things to his inferior?
5 Who brought the Feudal System to Britain?
6 When did it reach Scotland?
7 How did it differ from the Celtic ways?
8 Did it help the common people in any way?

Towns
1 Where did the new Burghs appear?
2 What were they for?
3 How did these towns differ from today's towns?
4 How did the King arrange for a new burgh to be set up?
5 What was it that Scotland had just developed which made burghs a good idea from the King's point of view?
6 Name some of these early burghs?
7 What town in Scotland has the oldest surviving charter?
8 What benefits did the people who set up house in a town get and what duties had they to perform?

Town Life
1 How would you describe the street scene in these ancient burghs?
2 What particular disaster was dreaded by the townsfolk?
3 What special duties and laws were there to help prevent this disaster?
4 When did the markets take place and who attended?
5 What kind of goods were traded in the market stalls?
6 How did the annual fair differ from ordinary market days?
7 Was all this trade taking place within Scotland or were there imports and exports too?
8 Why did the villagers always do their trading on the market days?

Tolls and Guilds
1 By what means did the King get his share of the new wealth?
2 Did all the new wealth come from within Scotland?
3 What was the main interest of those who lived in the towns?
4 How did they make themselves strong enough to protect their rights?
5 How did the guilds look after their members?
6 What part did the guilds play in the running of the town?
7 Did the guilds have anything to do with the price of goods and their quality?
8 What new body of people now took an active part in the affairs of the kingdom?

Building the Abbeys and Monasteries
1 Apart from castles, what other large buildings were now being built in Scotland by King David I?
2 What kind of craftsmen were required for the building of abbeys?
3 What was the first stage in the construction work?
4 Where were the great abbeys being built?
5 How was the roof of the abbey supported and what prevented its weight pushing the slim walls outwards?
6 How were the windows made?
7 Who was allowed into the most holy parts of the church?
8 How had the simple Celtic church changed?

Use Your Imagination

1 The sons of Malcolm Canmore and Margaret carried out great building projects. How do you think these affected the lives of ordinary peasant people?

2 What were the main features of the design that the Norman builders used for their castles? Draw a diagram.

3 The early castles were built of wood on a man-made hill. Do you think a stone castle could be built on the same type of mound?

4 What was the bailey and what activities went on within its protection?

5 Why do you suppose castles were not built of stone right away?

6 Are there any ways in which the peasant serfs would have found life better under the Normans, even if they had lost their freedom?

7 What great change did the Normans make which affects how most people live today?

8 What were the important features that made a good site for a town?

9 See if you can think of ways in which modern towns show their early Norman beginnings.

10 In what ways do you think the Normans caused the Scots to divide into two nations – Highlanders and Lowlanders?

Further Work

1 Imagine you are a peasant in Norman Scotland and you have come upon the building site of a great new castle. You watch the work from your hiding place and report all you have seen when you return to your village. Write a note of what you would tell your friends (Remember – you probably don't know what is being built.)

2 For a peasant who had always lived in a mud covered hovel, the sight of a new abbey must have been truly amazing. Try to remember a time when you were amazed by the size and beauty of something you were taken to see. See if you can write a poem about how it must have felt for these ancient peasants. Think of the shining stone and the soaring spire which seems to move as the clouds pass by, think of the glowing windows and beautiful doors, of the sound of singing and bells ringing . . .
The poem could be a list of answers to the question – 'What is an Abbey'

> An abbey is the peal of bells
> from tall pointed spires,
> The voice of singing
> through open windows
> That is what an abbey is.
>
> An abbey is . . .
> And so on

Add as many verses as you can think of.

3 Make a chart showing the feudal system, starting from the King at the top and working down. Illustrate the chart with drawings of the different ranks, showing their clothing and work.

4 Castles were designed not only to make it very difficult for attackers to force an entry but also easy for people to live inside and withstand siege, if necessary. Water supply and food would be just as important as a strong door which attackers cannot easily reach. See if your group can design a *very bad* castle with lots of mistakes and then show your plans to another group. Can they spot the weaknesses?

Border Business

David's Ambitions

Not all of King David's energies were spent in the building of churches and royal burghs. He also had dreams and ambitions about extending his kingdom. His wife was heir to the lands of Northumbria in the north of England which gave their only son, Prince Henry, good claim to be Earl of Northumbria. Scottish kings had long nursed the belief that this part of England was rightfully theirs. Now David could say with some truth that it was. Now he could march south under the banner of his wife's Saxon family and demand Northumbria for his son as the rightful Earl.

Civil War in England

But King David did not. For half his reign he made no move. Perhaps it was because of the friendship he felt for the King of England. But in the winter of 1135 King Henry I died. His throne was claimed by both Matilda, his daughter, and Stephen, her cousin. The civil war in England which followed was to last nineteen years. Sometimes Stephen was in control, at others Matilda gained the upper hand. King David was quick to take advantage of the unrest south of the border. Within weeks of the death of Henry I, David moved south in force. He claimed to be acting in the cause of the newly crowned Stephen and seized Carlisle and Newcastle. His real intentions were clear enough and soon King Stephen rode north at the head of a powerful army. The two kings met at Durham and after two weeks of argument and bargaining the Scots kept Carlisle and withdrew their army—but not King David's claim to Northumbria. Stephen promised that Prince Henry would have the Earldom.

Key towns in the Border dispute

Berwick
Roxburgh
Jedburgh
Dumfries
Wark
Newcastle upon Tyne
Carlisle
Hexham
Durham
Middlesbrough
Ripon
Lancaster
York
Leeds
Hull

King David invades the North of England

When, after two more years, King Stephen had failed to keep his word David went to war once more. In the spring of 1138 he opened his campaign. South he marched with a great army and a new just cause. This time it was in the name of the other rival, Matilda, that he led his spearmen from Galloway and the Lothians, his fierce Gaels from the Western Isles and his mounted Norman knights in their grey mail. With banners flying and weapons flashing under a bright sun the mighty column pushed down through Northumbria and Durham, down into Lancashire and Yorkshire. Nothing seemed able to resist them.

To those who watched it seemed that David King of Scots had come to conquer all England. On June 10th at Clitheroe, eleven or so miles north of Blackburn, a detachment of the great army drove from the field a defending English force. Castles fell one by one before the King's victorious march.

York from the air

Archbishop Thurstan

In the face of King David's crushing advance there dared to stand one very old and very brave man. His name was Thurstan and he was Archbishop of York. Outraged by the collapse of his country's defences, the old man called upon common folk and lords alike in the name of God to take up arms and brace themselves against the invaders. From hamlet and hall they flocked to his side and under summer skies marched north, their army growing day by day, till at last they faced the intruders at Northallerton. There the Archbishop raised his standard, the mast of a ship bearing a cross and the flags of St Peter, St John and St Wilfrid. From behind their barbed wall of shield and spear English voices swelled in the singing of psalms. To Thurstan's men it would be a holy war that they would fight that day.

The Battle of the Standard

From the very beginning things went ill for David's army. Having already lost to the other side a large number of his Norman knights a quarrel developed between those who remained loyal and the proud and fierce men of Galloway. The Galwegians claimed as their right the honour of leading the first attack even though they were without armour or any proper protection. Whether or not David consented or even gave the order to attack they hurled themselves forward in a hopeless charge to perish on the steady English spears and under a deadly rain of arrows.

When David saw the defeat and rout of the Galwegians he called up the men of Lothian and the Norman knights. In the face of this fierce new attack the English lines broke and victory was within David's grasp. Yet again events turned against him. A severed head was thrust aloft on an English spear and the cry went up that King David was dead. Without a king to fight for there seemed no purpose in the struggle and the Scots retreated. The bewildered David could not rally his forces and in the confusion of defeat would have dismounted to die there on the field had not his knights persuaded him to leave with his fleeing army. The Scottish soldiers were spared the usual hunt and slaughter probably because the Norman knights on the English side had a mind to the large estates they held and might lose in Scotland.

20

Divided Loyalties

King David's men, tired from months in the field, and many miles from home, felt no such enthusiasm to fight. Many of the great Scottish Norman knights were uncertain why they should fight at all. They had no quarrel with their kinsmen south of the border and little respect or affection for the native peoples who occupied Scotland, with whom they now marched. They tried to persuade David to change his mind and come to some bargain without fighting. When he would not, many of them, including some of the most important, promptly changed sides.

They also had a mind to the large estates they held and might lose in England. But nothing would divert David. If he must fight without them then he would. If he must fight against them then he would. On August 22nd 1138, battle was joined—the Battle of the Standard.

The Death of David

Though King David had lost the war at the Battle of the Standard he still managed to win the peace. Rather than risk further encounters with David's men, King Stephen renewed his promise of Northumbria for Prince Henry. The Scottish King returned to Edinburgh with his ambition fulfilled. The border now ran from Derwent Water in the west to the River Tyne in the east.

But not for long. In 1153, Prince Henry died. Months later, still in mourning, King David came to the end of his own life. He was succeeded by Malcolm, his twelve year old grandson. By the time the boy king was sixteen he had returned Northumbria to the English King, who had impressed Malcolm with the strength of his arguments and with the strength of his army too! In the face of so much strength it seemed the prudent thing to do.

The Border Established

The border never really moved south again though the kings that followed Malcolm pressed hard to regain Northumbria for the Scottish Crown. Malcolm's brother, William the Lion, came to the throne in 1165 and spent much of the next half century trying to win back the lost lands of north England. He failed—but he did give to Scotland the emblem which he had chosen for his shield—a roaring clawing beast of blood red on a background of yellow—the Lion Rampant.

Alexander II

The seals of Alexander II

Alexander II followed his father to the throne in 1214. In 1237 he finally settled for lands in Northumbria worth two hundred pounds a year. Lands—but no castles, and without castles the power stayed firmly in the English King's hands. Northumbria stayed firmly in England. But the southward push of determined Scottish kings had not been without value. The rich farm lands that lie between the Solway–Tweed line and the old remains of the Antonine wall have stayed safely in Scotland despite the interest shown in them by powerful rulers of England.

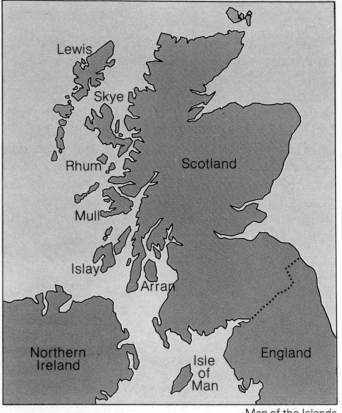

Map of the Islands

The Islands

Scotland had other borders to the north and west where the Isles had been held by the King of Norway since the days when King Edgar lost them. The chiefs who ruled there took little enough notice of kings, Norwegian or Scottish and in 1230 King Haakon sent a powerful force of his Norsemen to bring them to heel. They landed on the island of Bute and took Rothesay Castle by hacking their way with axes straight through its soft sandstone walls, their shields held overhead to ward off the missiles and boiling pitch hurled down on them from the battlements.

It occurred to King Alexander that such unruly places might be unwanted by King Haakon if he could be rid of them at a profit, so he made an offer to buy the Western Isles from the Norwegians. When his offer was refused he made up his mind to take by force what he could not have peacefully. Having just crushed two rebellions in Galloway he turned his eyes to the north-west and in 1249 sailed with his fleet to claim the islands there for Scotland. But he died aboard his ship in Oban Bay before his campaign could properly begin. It would be the task of his son to bring the Western Isles within the borders of Scotland.

Alexander III

Alexander III was only eight when on the 13th July 1249, he mounted the Stone of Destiny in the presence of the great nobles and churchmen. A king cannot rule as a child, and so for ten years regents jealously squabbled among themselves over the government of the land. The noisy quarrelling was ended and Alexander gained some peace when they finally agreed to allow the affairs of the kingdom to be controlled by a grand council of powerful lords—all chosen by the King of England.

The Fight for the Western Isles

Alexander III was twenty-one when he began his own rule by taking up the fight for the Western Isles which his father's death in Oban Bay had left unfinished. First he renewed the offer to buy the islands but King Haakon was now older and even less willing to accept. This time, however, someone else took a hand in the business. The Earl of Ross, one of Alexander's nobles, attacked the Isle of Skye. Angered by this warlike act, King Haakon grew determined to put an end to any ideas the Scottish King might have of seizing his island dominions.

Norwegians attacking Rothesay Castle

King Haakon sails for Scotland

On the 11th July 1263, he sailed from Norway. Haakon had more than a hundred and fifty longships, led by his own proud and mighty vessel. Its fearsome dragons of gold at prow and sternpost rose and fell as it pressed through the grey water. After the first leg of their journey the ships anchored in the shelter of Kirkwall bay in the Isles of Orkney. There Haakon hoped to raise more support for his great expedition but in this he was to be disappointed. To make matters worse something strange and very disturbing happened while the fleet rested and made preparations at Kirkwall. August 5th was a clear summer day and the Norsemen were busy at their work when suddenly the midday sun vanished from the sky leaving only a rim of brightness and chill darkness crept over the land. The cold shadow passed, the sun returned but a troubled army was left that knew nothing of eclipses and strongly believed in bad omens.

The Norwegian fleet left Orkney on the 10th August and moved south down the west coast of Scotland. Once again the seaward sky was filled with the dragonships of the Norsemen. The old dread chilled the minds and hearts of the common folk and half-forgotten prayers were muttered fearfully. The Vikings had come again.

King Alexander III waited in tense readiness. All the way down the west coast his ships shadowed the great fleet. Royal messengers spurred their mounts overland to bring news of the movements and worrying reports of its growing strength. King Magnus of Man had joined forces with Haakon in the Sound of Skye. And there was news of raiding parties too, on the Mull of Kintyre, and Bute where Rothesay Castle had fallen.

King Haakon

Norwegian arrow heads

King Alexander's Plan

By late August the Norwegian fleet had rounded the Isle of Arran and lay at anchor in Lamlash Bay, sheltering behind the Holy Isle and making final preparations. On the mainland the Scottish King marched his army to the Burgh of Ayr, founded by his grandfather. There he waited and watched. Only twenty miles separated the two forces and Alexander was troubled. There was however one further step he could take. It was now into September and the summer was dying. An army at sea might well have more than one enemy to face if the weather should break. Time was on the side of the Scottish King. He stalled the invaders. Under a flag of truce a party of barefooted Dominican monks carried Alexander's terms for peace to King Haakon. The discussion dragged on for days. Every day Alexander's army grew, and there was more chance that the weather would fail.

By late September the delaying tactics were over and the invaders moved in for the attack. Up the Firth of Clyde they sailed; the Scots defenders braced themselves for what must surely come. Suddenly and from nowhere, on the first of October, the storm struck. The proud fleet of King Haakon was tossed about helplessly on the surging waves by winds that tore ships from their anchor, lines and rigging from the masts. Some vessels foundered at sea, some were swept on to the beaches below the slopes of the Cunningham Hills at Largs—which means 'the slopes.'

Discussing the truce.   **right:** Largs from the air

The Battle of Largs

Some sort of fighting between small detachments of the two forces took place that Monday morning and on the Tuesday. Volleys of aimless arrows were exchanged and each side made uncertain charges up and down the beaches. The sight of the Scottish King's army assembling in full battle array under the command of Alexander Stewart, convinced the Norwegians that their task was now hopeless. They withdrew in good order and sailed down river to regroup once more in Lamlash Bay from where they set sail homeward. King Haakon died in the early hours of Sunday, 16th December 1263, in the Bishop's Palace, while his fleet wintered at Kirkwall.

The Battle of Largs hardly happened at all yet it was an important victory for King Alexander III. Within three years King Magnus, the son of Haakon, returned the Western Isles to the Scottish Crown—not that the island chiefs would pay much heed to that. The kingdom of Scotland's western border had now been settled and only the cold grey Atlantic lay beyond.

Worksection

Border Business
Understand Your Work

Ambitions

1 Why did King David believe he had a good claim to Northumbria?
2 How long did he wait before trying to force his claim on Northumbria?
3 What did he pretend to be doing, when he marched into England?
4 How did King Stephen settle the claim?
5 What caused David to go to war again?
6 Who put up a fight against the armies of King David?
7 What finally decided the Battle of the Standard?
8 Did David fail in his ambition?

The Border

1 Did the Scots manage to move the border southwards?
2 Find out where the Scottish English border runs?
3 What is William the Lion remembered for?
4 In what direction did King Alexander III try to extend his kingdom?
5 Against whom did he have to fight?
6 What upset the Norsemen while sheltering in Kirkwall bay?
7 How did the ordinary folk feel when they saw the Viking fleet.
8 How did King Alexander know what the invading fleet was doing?

The Battle of Largs

1 Where did the Norwegian fleet gather support and from whom?
2 What castle fell to the Norsemen?
3 Where was the invading fleet anchored in late August 1263?
4 How did King Alexander try to gain an advantage over King Haakon's army?
5 Where and how did the Norwegian fleet run into trouble?
6 What did the invading fleet do when faced by the Scottish Army at Largs?
7 What does 'Largs' mean?
8 As a result of the battle what territory did the Scottish crown recover?

Use Your Imagination

1 Why do you think the battle at Northallerton on August 22 1138 is called the Battle of the Standard?
2 What feelings do you suppose made David's men less willing to fight than the men of Archbishop Thurston?
3 What do you think caused King Stephen to allow David to 'win the peace' after he had lost the Battle of the Standard?
4 Trace on a map where you think the Scottish–English border ran at the end of David's reign. Compare this with the present border.
5 What do you imagine the common folk in the sea-side villages did when they caught sight of King Haakon's Viking fleet?
6 Why do you think King Alexander III delayed the battle with King Haakon for as long as he could?
7 What was the real cause of the Norwegians' retreat from the Battle of Largs?
8 What made this an important victory for the Scottish King?
9 Find Arran and Largs on a map of the west of Scotland. Trace the crossing that King Haakon made.
10 Why do you think that the winning back of the Western Isles may not have been a great help to the Scottish Crown?

Further Work

1 Here is a little poem by Carl Sandburg. Read it and see if it helps you to understand why powerful people built castles:

> Get off this estate,
> What for?
> Because it's mine.
> Where did you get it?
> From my father.
> And where did he get it?
> From his father.
> And where did he get it?
> He fought for it.
> Well, I'll fight you for it.

2 William the Lion introduced the Lion Rampant as the Scottish flag. Find a picture of it and make an accurate copy. Find out what you can about the flags of England, Ireland and Wales.

3 King Haakon's men were upset by the sudden darkening of the midday sun. Find out what you can about eclipses, when and how they happen.

4 Try to imagine what the Viking warriors would have thought and said about the strange midday darkness. Some would think it a bad omen while others might say that it showed their King could conquer even the sun!

Discuss this in your group and see how many ideas you can think up for eclipses being good or bad omens. Your group could make up a little play to perform to the rest of the class.

5 Write a story about how someone used an eclipse to help him or her. Perhaps it was by pretending to be magic and able to blot out the sun or perhaps the sudden darkness helped an escape or. . . . Give your story a title and make a neat copy for others to read.

6 King Alexander wanted to delay the Norwegian attack for as long as possible. Why do you think this helped the Scottish King and what do you suppose the Dominican monks, who carried Alexander's peace terms, might have done to waste as much time as possible? Think of some ideas which might cause King Haakon to consider them seriously. Write your terms for peace to delay the Norsemen.

7 Imagine you are on your first visit to a market day in the new royal burgh. How do you feel? What do you see, hear, smell? What do you think about it all? What happens? Write a story about this.

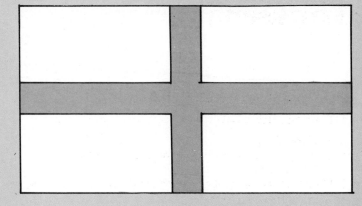

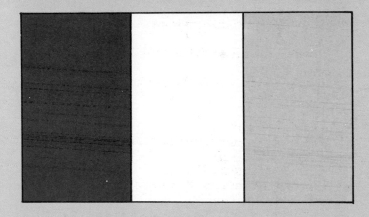

The Golden Years

The Land

The land ruled by King Alexander III was still a place given more to forest and marsh than to open pasture or rich farmland. Wild beasts roamed the countryside—grey wolves, charging boars, herds of red deer and white cattle. The waterways teemed with silver darting fish and the stillness overhead was shattered by the sudden cries of wildfowl. It was still a wet and windswept kingdom though the weather then was the best Scotland has ever enjoyed. To some it was the end of the earth however, and from Rome it was only reached after two months of wearying travel.

Changes

But there had been changes too. Now a network of the King's highways ran the length and breadth of the country joining the Royal Burghs, of which there were more than fifty, and linking with the castles too. Getting about was easier now and though a day's journey on horseback rarely bettered twenty miles, in emergencies, with relays of fresh fast mounts, something like a hundred miles might be expected on the hard packed surfaces of the new highways. Rivers were still the best travel ways. Sea going ships came up to Stirling on the Forth and to Perth on the Tay but, on the shallow Clyde, only as far as Dumbarton. Rivers could be crossed now by bridge or ferry—the Forth at Stirling and Airth, Queensferry and Earlsferry; the Tay at Perth and the Tweed at both Roxburgh and Berwick.

Scotland's major ports

Castles

Castles of the period were mostly wooden towers perched high on man made hills and stoutly defended by ditch, fence and stern faced men in their grey suits of chain-mail. But some were built of stone—Rothesay Castle on the Isle of Bute and Dirleton in East Lothian a mile or two west of where North Berwick now stands; Kildrummy Castle in Aberdeenshire where the Don loops east before swinging west to flow into the North Sea and the mighty tower of Bothwell on the Clyde, with its smooth and perfect stonework; and others too. They were huge strongholds of outer and inner walls and towers rising sheer from deep dark moats to heights greater than twenty metres (nearer thirty at Bothwell) and five in thickness. Over the narrow span of the drawbridge, ready to be raised at a moment's alarm, the way led through a massive gatehouse to the towering keep. Here, in the great hall, the Lord with his Lady enjoyed the power and riches of a feudal baron, feasting at their raised table and listening to the songs and tales of minstrels, perhaps after a day at the tournament or delighting in the hunt of bird and beast over the wide estates and now sparser forests.

Country Life

But mostly the people of Scotland lived very close to the earth from which came their meagre share of wealth. Their little townships and lonely farmsteads were spread over the kingdom wherever the ground was good. Only in the baron's court, where disputes were settled and work planned, did these peasant farmers find a kind of village community centre.

There were perhaps as many country folk in Scotland then as there are today but their methods of farming were very different. The croplands were ploughed in long narrow strips called rigs. Great wooden ploughs were heaved and guided through the stubborn soil by teams of eight oxen and as many men. The land was measured by the area such a team could cultivate yearly. It was called a ploughgate and usually amounted to something over one hundred acres, just enough to keep a village in work and food.

The croplands were usually on the hillside and were ploughed up and down the slope. Between the rigs, which at most were only ten paces wide, long ditches were dug. The soil was heaped up on the rigs to raise their level and to improve their quality. The ditches collected the rainwater from the rigs and drained it downhill

preventing the ground from becoming waterlogged in the wet Scottish weather. Good as it was for sloping ground this drainage system was not successful on the rich but flat riverside lands. These remained marshy, grazed by the herds while ox and man toiled on the hillside.

But it was livestock more than crops that provided life support for the people—cattle in the highlands and sheep in the lowlands. In the summer, herds and flocks were driven to new pastures usually on higher ground. There the men guarded them against wolf and fox, and there the sheep were sheared. The womenfolk spun the new wool, and made butter and cheese from the milk of cow and ewe. These summer pastures and the shelters built upon them were called shielings.

In mid November, as the first chill of coming winter was felt, most of the beasts had to be slaughtered. Only a few were kept, for plough teams, breeding and to give milk. There was simply not enough food to see them through the long dark months. Their carcasses were preserved in salt and, until spring, the only fresh meat for the people would be from hunting. The only change in their diet would be oatmeal, barley-bread and salt herring. Famine was never far from the minds of the people and the struggle to survive used all their time and all their energy. Only the strongest would succeed.

A countryman's diet

Fuel

Forests, thinned over the centuries, still provided logs for the great hearth in the castle hall, but others made do with peat cut from the vast areas of bog that still covered much of the land. More recently another fuel was burning in the open fires of peasant cottages. It was first found scattered amongst the stones on the shore and later dug out from the sea-cliff face by the monks of Newbattle Abbey. It was called 'black stone' long before it became better known as 'coal'.

St. Magnus today

The Church

The Church was now more than ever involved in practical business matters—sheep farming, the commercial production of salt by boiling off salt water, property owning and trade. That it was strong and rich could be seen from the great buildings of its abbeys and monsteries. But comfort and help for the poor came mainly from the parish priest whose simple life was closer to the people in their squat hovels of mud and turf and closer to a true holiness than the rich living of many of those behind the monastery walls.

And something else had come to Scotland during the reign of King Alexander III, something which had never really been tried before, an experiment called peace. For the first time the people of Scotland enjoyed an age when there was no threat of war from outside its borders, a golden age when the kingdom prospered.

Reconstruction of 12th century church of St. Magnus in Orkney

The Death of Prince Alexander

But it was not to last. The first hint of approaching trouble came on 17th January 1284, when Prince Alexander, heir to the throne and only surviving child of the King, died after a long illness and within a week of his twenty-first birthday. On his deathbed the young prince is said to have foretold that his uncle King Edward I of England would attack Scotland three times 'Twice he will conquer, in the third he will be overthrown.'

Of course people told themselves that no such thing could happen while King Alexander ruled the land. Edward was his friend and dearest brother-in-law. They put the matter behind them and set about the business of finding another heir. It was little Margaret of Norway the Grand Council chose. She was one year old and grand-daughter of the King—but most would have preferred a strong boy in good health to wear his father's crown when the time came.

There was a moment's break in the gathering clouds in the autumn of 1285 when the King remarried and there was once more the bright hope that there might yet be such a boy.

An Error of Judgment

On Monday 18th March, only five months after his wedding, the King was at Edinburgh Castle with his high council. The new queen had remained at Kinghorn. Business concluded, Alexander decided, over a glass of wine or two, that he would return to his young wife that night. Outside, the wind that had been gusting strongly all day was now of gale force and from the north. The skies were overcast and there was snow in the air. When he rose from the table it was already dusk and twenty miles of rough track and sea ferry lay between him and the manor where Queen Yolande waited. His lords of the council earnestly advised him not to attempt the journey. The boatman at Queensferry told him bluntly that crossing the two miles of grey Forth would be folly. With equal bluntness he was advised against travel and invited to weather the storm in the homes of burgesses in both Dalmeny on the south shore and Inverkeithing on the north. Alexander pressed on. In the heavy winds and deepening gloom he became separated from his guides and small escort to vanish in the darkness. The following morning Alexander III, King of Scots, was found dead of a broken neck on the shore beneath the sea cliff over which his horse had stumbled. All too suddenly the kingdom had for its leader a little girl in far off Norway.

One Nation

The Guardians

Alexander III was dead and the heir apparent to the Scottish throne was Margaret the little Princess of Norway. Towards the end of April 1286 the great men of the land, earls and barons, bishops and abbots, met at Scone to put in order the affairs of state. It was only a week or two since the funeral of the King at Dunfermline but there was great need for haste. The first danger to peace could well come from within the kingdom. There were others who felt they had a claim to the crown.

The members of this grand council of Scone first swore a solemn oath to be loyal and constant in the service of the three year old Princess; to preserve her kingdom and to keep her peace. The realm, they agreed, should be governed in her name by six guardians chosen from the council. For the north, above the Forth, there would be Bishop Fraser of St. Andrews; Alexander Comyn, Earl of Buchan; and Duncan MacDuff the young Earl of Fife. For the south, Bishop Wishart of Glasgow; John Comyn, Lord of Badenoch; and James the High Steward, Baron of Renfrew.

In early August the guardians sent three envoys to King Edward I of England to seek his advice and assistance. They returned before the end of the year with the news that Edward would help—at a price. He insisted on being recognised as the overlord of Scotland. It was a price the guardians could not willingly pay. Then, in Galloway, the Lord of Annandale, with his son the Earl of Carrick, raised an army to press his own claim to the throne.

The trouble was settled peaceably, for the moment, but the family in Annandale and Carrick had served notice of its strong interest in the Scottish Crown, a family brought to Scotland by David I; a family called Bruce.

A Marriage Treaty

However, there still seemed to be hope, even joy in the kingdom during the summer of 1290. By the end of August, King Edward had confirmed plans for the future marriage of his son and heir, the Prince Edward of Caernarvon to Margaret heir of Scotland. And yet the clouds had not completely cleared. Not only did the King of England renew, in this marriage treaty, his claim to be overlord of Scotland, he took control of the Isle of Man, a possession of the Scottish Crown, without bothering to consult the guardians. But the promised union in marriage of the heirs to the kingdoms would surely mean peace and friendship just as there had been under Alexander III. There was good reason for the guardians to feel well pleased with their work.

The Maid of Norway

As summer turned to autumn, the Maid of Norway, now six, left Bergen for the protection of the Royal Court in England. Her future marriage with the heir to the English throne promised a kind of united Britain free from mistrust and border war. On that voyage of hope during the first days of October 1290, she took ill and died in the Isles of Orkney. Now there was no known heir to the throne and many who would claim it.

To the south lay a powerful neighbour with a powerful king who more than once had claimed the right to be Overlord of Scotland. Already Bruce of Annandale was on the march towards Perth. Already John Balliol was calling himself 'heir of Scotland.' One of the guardians, Bishop Fraser of St. Andrews, acted with great speed writing once again to the English King begging him to come to the people of Scotland and 'to save the shedding of blood, and to set over them for King, who, of right, ought to have the succession'. And Edward came.

King Edward at Berwick

He came to Berwick Castle but not until 2nd August 1291, and not until he had taken certain precautions. Edward would judge who as 'of right' should rule Scotland amongst the thirteen who claimed the honour—but he would do it his way. He came with an army ready for the field and a navy ready for action. He came ready for talk or war.

Again Edward had repeated his claim to be Lord Superior of Scotland. The Scots said that while they knew Edward would never ask such a thing unless he really believed it to be proper, they, without a king, could not give an answer. Outwitted by this move the English King changed his tactics and asked each of the would-be Kings to accept him as overlord. Not wishing to spoil their chances in the competition for the throne, they all agreed. He also convinced them and the guardians too that the royal castles should be held in his hands so that he could deliver them to the man he chose for king. So Edward had the castles of Scotland and the future king in his power before the work began.

Edward's Choice

The whole business dragged on for more than a year in the great hall of Berwick Castle. A court of one hundred and four barons, earls and men of the Church watched over by Edward, heard no fewer than thirteen claims for the Scottish throne. In the end just two of the thirteen—Bruce of Annandale, the first grandson of the second granddaughter of David I, and John Balliol, the second grandson of the first granddaughter of David, were left. On 17th November 1292, Edward found in favour of John Balliol. On the day following the award he fell on his knees before the English King and did homage to him. He began his rule with the warning ringing in his ears that he should govern justly or else the Lord Superior of Scotland would apply a guiding hand. The message was clear enough. King John was a puppet who would dance on royal strings held firmly in Edward's powerful hand.

Berwick castle today

John Balliol's Coat of Arms

right: King John's document of surrendering the realm to Edward, 1296

below: John Balliol kneels in hommage before Edward I

King John

It was to be a miserable reign of four shameful years that King John and Scotland would endure. Success was made impossible by supporters of the defeated claimants and by the humiliating demands of the King of England. It was all intended to show that King John was no King at all, that Scotland was no kingdom, only a kind of feudal barony of England.

Unrest and anger was growing in Scotland, fed by the insults hurled against the kingdom by Edward. It flared into action when the English King ordered the Scots to fight for him against the French. Instead they joined with France. So began a lasting friendship between the two countries. At the time it caused Edward to turn his full fury on Scotland. He marched north and entered Scotland at Coldstream on 28th March 1296, and two days later seized Berwick burning and killing without mercy. King John had had enough. He withdrew his homage from Edward which he declared had only been given under force in the

first place and made ready to face the might of England in war.

But Scotland was no match for England's larger, better equipped and better paid army led by the great heavy cavalry of the knights. King John's own army was routed at Dunbar a month after the fall of Berwick and castles fell one after the other to Edward, Dunbar itself and Roxburgh, Jedburgh, Dumbarton and the great castle of Edinburgh after only a week's siege.

King John Surrenders

On 2nd July 1296, King John surrendered to Edward at Kincardine Castle, confessing his guilt and giving over to Edward his land and his people. He then suffered the final shame of having his crown taken from his head, the royal sceptre dragged from his grasp, the ring pulled from his finger and the ermine and coat of arms ripped from his tabard. He was then taken as a prisoner to the Tower of London. King John had lost his kingdom and found a nickname by which his shame would be forever remembered—Toom Tabard (empty coat), which meant King Nobody.

The English in Scotland

Edward carried the Royal Standard of England as far north as it had ever been, right to Elgin, capital of Moray, but meeting no further resistance swung south again towards Berwick. On the return march he seized the ancient Stone of Destiny on which Kings of Scotland were crowned and sent it to Westminster Abbey. It was placed under the English throne, where it still remains. He took also the most sacred thing in the land, the Black Rood of St Margaret said to be made from the true cross itself. Any papers which showed that there ever had been a separate kingdom of the north were also removed.

Edward meant to humble Scotland, even to end its existence. Such was his contempt for the place and the people that he carelessly and deeply offended even those who would have supported him and had done so in the past. When the Earl of Carrick, a man of feeble spirit, asked if he would be King as the next in line to John Balliol he was sent packing, with the haughty rebuke 'Have we nothing better to do than win kingdoms for you?'

The Ragman Roll

The Stone of Scone underneath the British throne

Throughout the land earls and barons, bishops and leading burgesses were made to sign an oath of loyalty to King Edward of England. Thirty-five pages long, the document contained two thousand names. Because of the ragged tangle of ribbons hanging down from the wax seals it was called the Ragman Roll. By his stern insistence that Scotland should submit and become part of his kingdom, Edward brutally humbled the pride and dignity of the Scottish people. He failed to see that the loyalty he took by force was not worth the parchment on which the Ragman Roll was written. He failed to see that instead of putting down a rebel Scotland he had kindled a fire in its heart. Whatever differences they had amongst themselves the Scots now shared, as one people, a hatred of the English judges and tax collectors, the English soldiers and English castles that occupied their land. As one people they now desired freedom from England above all else.

The defeat of King John's army at Dunbar had broken the power of the Scottish barons and earls and brought them on their knees before Edward. But there were still the people themselves, landowners large and small, the freeholders and even the peasants. They could and would resist their harsh overlord from the south. From Pict and Scot, Angle and Briton, Norseman, Fleming and Norman, indeed from all who had settled in this northern place over the centuries since the ice had released the land from its freezing grip, there now came forth a nation.

Worksection

The Golden Years
Understand Your Work
The Land
1 What sort of countryside did King Alexander III rule over?
2 What made land travel between places easier then?
3 How quickly did people usually travel overland, and what was the fastest rate in an emergency?
4 What other improvements made land travel easier?
5 What was the best means of travel in Alexander's kingdom?
6 How were the weather conditions in Alexander's time?
7 What animals roamed the countryside?
8 What were connected by the network of the King's highways?

Castles
1 Where were stone castles to be found in Alexander's Scotland?
2 How did they differ from the wooden structures?
3 How was the approach to the castle gateway made very difficult?
4 What kind of life was led by the Lord of the castle and his Lady?
5 How was their importance shown as they feasted in the great hall of their castle?
6 What entertainments took place in the castle?
7 Why were the forests becoming sparser?
8 What were the favourite outdoor sports of the Lord and his Lady?

Country Life
1 How did most of Scotland's people live in the 13th century?
2 How did the number of country folk in Scotland under Alexander III compare with the number today?
3 What name was given to the long narrow fields in which the crops grew?
4 What was a ploughgate?
5 Why were the rigs usually on the hillside?
6 The flat riverside lands were rich and fertile. Why were they not farmed?
7 What man and animal power was needed to coax the wooden ploughs through the heavy soil?
8 What jobs were undertaken by the womenfolk during the summer months?
9 When winter came most of the beasts were slaughtered. Why were some kept alive?
10 What was the winter diet of the country folk?
11 What new fuel was supplied from Newbattle Abbey?
12 How was the Church now involved in the business matters of the country?
13 Who did the day to day work of the Church, comforting the sick and helping the poor?
14 What was the greatest benefit the ordinary folk enjoyed during Alexander III's reign?

The End of the Golden Age
1 What prophecy is Alexander's son, the heir to the throne, believed to have made on his death bed?
2 Why did the people think this could not happen?
3 Who was chosen to succeed Alexander III to the throne?
4 What happened in 1285 that made things seem brighter for a time?
5 Where was the King travelling to on the 18th March 1286?
6 What was the result of that journey?
7 Find on a map the route he followed?
8 Why and by whom had the King been advised against making the trip?

One Nation
The Guardians
1 What danger was to be faced after the King's sudden death?
2 How was the kingdom to be governed until the Maid of Norway was old enough to take her throne?
3 Who were the people chosen to rule?
4 From where did they seek assistance and what was to be the price of this?
5 What King of Scotland had encouraged the English King to think that he was Overlord of the King of Scots?
6 What happened in October 1290 which upset the Guardians' plans for Scotland?
7 What began to happen in Scotland then?
8 How did the Guardians 'save the shedding of blood'?

King Nobody
1 Did Edward I of England arrive at once to help the Scots?
2 Did he come in peace or in force?
3 How was his claim to be Overlord of Scotland rejected?
4 What steps did Edward take to make sure he would control Scotland?
5 Whom did King Edward choose to rule Scotland?
6 What caused King John Balliol to withdraw his homage to Edward?
7 How was the Scottish King dealt with for his resistance to England?
8 What nickname was given to the Scottish King in disgrace?

The English in Scotland
1 How far north did the English army march to subdue Scotland?
2 What famous items were seized by the English King during this campaign?
3 What was Edward trying to do?
4 How did he try to ensure the loyalty of all the important people in Scotland?
5 How many names appeared on the document called the Ragman Roll?
6 Why was it so called?

7 Did Edward's plan to bring Scotland under his control work well?

8 How did the actions of the English King help to make the Scottish Nation?

Use Your Imagination

1 How would you describe the length of a journey or the distance between towns in the time of King Alexander III?

2 Why were river crossings good places to set up a new royal burgh?

3 What were the two main types of occupation that people had in towns? For example a blacksmith was one type and a cloth merchant another.

4 How do you think the walls of a castle might be designed to allow the defenders to drive off attackers who are hard up against the walls? Remember, if the defenders look over they will be easy targets for the archers. Draw a plan of your idea.

5 How was salt obtained?

6 Why do you think the rigs were long and narrow?

7 Do you think Alexander's reign was a Golden Age for the common folk?

8 Why do you think the people who claimed the Scottish throne agreed to the condition that they would accept Edward I as their overlord? Do you suppose they intended to keep this promise?

9 Why did Edward need to hold the Scottish castles?

10 Do you think Edward I was wise in taking revenge on Scotland to the extent he did? Could you suggest a better policy?

Further Work

1 How do you suppose it was discovered that coal could burn? Make up a story about how you think this came about? It can be one which could have happened or a 'magic-type' legend or whatever you like.

2 Write a group song which would tell a story to the Baron and his Lady. You can make up your own tune or use an existing one. It might be wise if it says something nice about the courage and goodness of the Baron!

3 Prepare a group play about the King and his fateful Journey to Kinghorn. Each member of your group can think up reasons why the King should not go out in the storm. The play should begin with the King still at the table in Edinburgh Castle. When the play is over, discuss what you think may have caused the King to make such a mistake against all the advice he received.

4 King Alexander made an error of judgment when he set out on the journey to Kinghorn. Can you think of any reason his judgment may have been less good than usual? Are there many things which might affect a person's judgment? Discuss this with your group and make a list of things to be avoided when important decisions are to be made.

5 Well designed stone castles were very difficult to take. The walls were too thick and too high. Can you think of ways to get inside a castle that is too strong to storm? See what kind of tricks your group can invent.

6 Edward I of England tried to humble the Scots and force them to pay homage. Was this the best way to keep control and to win loyalty? If you had been in his position what steps might you have taken to hold your position as Overlord of Scotland?

7 Of the important items taken to England by Edward, the Stone of Destiny is the one which has interested Scots most. In recent years it was seized by a group of young Scots but later found and returned to Westminster Abbey. See if you can find out more about this story.

The Freedom Fighters

Edward and Scotland

Everybody in England could recite an old rhyme which ran,

'If that you will France win,
 Then with Scotland first begin.'

King Edward was a proud and brutal soldier and he could never forget or forgive the friendship John Balliol and the Scots had offered his enemies—for his main ambitions were in France. He could not safely take his main forces overseas whilst Scotland threatened his 'back door'. Indeed, this may not have been what Scotland threatened, but what mattered was what Edward feared. So Scotland, by the end of the thirteenth century, was an occupied country ruled over by its powerful neighbour in the south. The will to fight amongst its great nobles had been crushed at the Battle of Dunbar on the 27th April 1296. Edward had even forced from them a pledge, sealed on the parchment sheets of the **Ragman Roll**, that they would remain forever his good and loyal servants. There was then no Kingdom of Scotland, only a place belonging to the English Crown with the English King for Lord Superior. Resistance was broken. All the north was Edward's, just as he had always wanted.

That, at least, is what the King of England firmly believed when in September, he left Scotland for another war—this time with France. And he had good reason for his high hopes. In those days it was kings and princes, barons and earls who quarrelled over countries. Kingdoms belonged to such people or, at least, to those amongst them who proved to be the strongest. The common folk just served whoever that turned out to be.

But Edward was wrong. He was twice wrong. Like the Roman Emperor Domitian who, twelve centuries before, had recalled Agricola too soon, Edward mistook the defeat of an army for the defeat of the people. He supposed that the people would take the surrender of their nobles as their own surrender and dutifully serve the King of England as their new overlord.

He made his second mistake when he harshly punished the Scottish people for daring to be a separate kingdom, for wanting to serve their own King. Not content with victory in battle he disgraced the whole realm seizing its most treasured and sacred things. He meant to teach Scotland a lesson that would never be forgotten. But just as people in Scotland were beginning to feel unitedly Scottish, so they were beginning to feel angry. Even if the nobles had accepted defeat, there were others who could and would carry on the fight. And there was a clue to this in Edward's Ragman Roll—or rather, not in it! It was a missing name. Not the name of a great baron or earl but one of knightly stock, certainly important enough to have been there.

Two brothers had refused to register their oaths of loyalty to a foreign King. The elder, Malcolm, was a landowner from Elderslie, near Paisley, and his brother was called William. Their family had come from Shropshire more than a century before, probably invited by David I. Their name meant simply, Welshman or Celt. It was spelled 'Waleys' or 'Walays' before it was better known as Wallace.

Castles in English hands

William Wallace

In a land smouldering with anger it needed only the arrival of a true leader to excite the people to revolt. In the May of 1297, William Wallace struck down the English Sheriff of Clydesdale, Sir William Hazelrig. The people rose to his call eager to throw off the harsh yoke placed on their necks by the English King and rebellion swept through the land with lightning speed.

The events which led to this fateful day had begun when Edward left Scotland in the previous September. He put its affairs in the hands of John de Warenne, Earl of Surrey, the victor of Dunbar. The Earl disliked Scotland and spent most of his time south of the border in his Yorkshire estates, leaving the day to day running of the country to the King's Treasurer, Hugh de Cressingham. He was a bad choice too. Cressingham was an ambitious unpleasant man desperate to push his ample bulk as high in his King's service and favour as he could climb. On that ladder Scotland was just another rung—but it would be a rung too high. He was hated by the Scottish people who called him not 'treasurer' but 'treacherer'.

Some arms and seals of those involved in the Rebellion.

While these two men were misunderstanding and mishandling Scotland, trouble was flaring here and there throughout the land. Wallace, for refusing to sign the Ragman Roll, had been made an outlaw. After a scuffle with English soldiers in Lanark he had only managed to escape with the help of his wife. For this Hazelrig had her put to death and their house burned to the ground. It was then that William Wallace, in revenge, struck down the English Sheriff. With that blow he became 'chief of brigands' and over the dead Hazelrig, called all Scotland to revolt. The answer came swiftly. People flocked to his banner and at the head of these freedom fighters—called brigands and outlaws by Edward—Wallace moved north to the mountains, there to plan his campaign.

The English Chief Justice, William de Ormsby, who had declared Wallace an outlaw,

Bothwell Castle

was busy at Scone declaring other Scots to be outlaws too for failing to swear loyalty to the English King. Without warning Wallace and his men attacked his court and Ormsby barely escaped with his life leaving all else as welcome booty for Wallace's men. He fled to Edinburgh bringing news of the rebellion which now burned across the country. North of the Forth, Wallace and his ragged band were daily growing stronger and more daring. Further north still, beyond the high ridge of the Mounth, in Moray, Banff and Aberdeen, another standard was raised in the cause of freedom. Andrew Murray, a young man like Wallace but the son of a baron, and heir to the great estates of Moray and the lordship of Bothwell, was rousing the Gaels to revolt. And in the south-west, Bishop Wishart of Glasgow and James the High Steward—both had been Guardians of the Realm—were gathering their strength to show just how flimsy was the parchment loyalty forced from them by Edward. They were joined by other nobles including the young Earl of Carrick who had always been faithful to Edward. Now he declared, 'No man holds his flesh and blood in hatred, and I am no exception. I must join my own people and the nation in which I was born.' The English King would have done well to heed the words of young Carrick, a man who would soon be better known as Robert Bruce.

Wallace is revenged on Hazelrig

Edward Strikes Back

The first counterstrike against the revolt was directed at these nobles. Edward still believed that if the nobility was brought to order the people must follow. An English army, raised in the border countries, marched swiftly north through Annandale and Nithsdale and reached the Royal Burgh of Ayr towards the end of June. The Scots waiting a few miles further north at Irvine were ill-prepared, and their leaders inexperienced—more a rabble than an army. The English were well practised in the business of conquest—crushing the Welsh, warring with France. When the Scots caught sight of the steady surge of approaching cavalry, heavily armoured, their great lances thrusting skywards with bright pennons flying, when they heard the hard clank of mail and the thunder of hooves, their hearts were chilled. Their leaders, seeing the hopelessness of the situation declined to fight.

Negotiations

But surrender was quite another matter. The Scottish nobles talked for almost a month with their high-sounding formal claims and counter claims. All this time they knew that Wallace and Murray were gathering strength. All this time castles were being retaken. English officials were being replaced by Scots. Steadily and surely Edward's henchmen were being swept out of the north by Murray. Inverness and Castle Urquhart were in his hands as he led his men in triumph down through Aberdeenshire. Steadily and surely they were being swept out of the south by Wallace whose growing force had Dundee Castle under siege.

The March to Stirling

At the end of the summer the two forces of freedom fighters met for the first time and marched together behind their two leaders towards Stirling. It was an army of common folk, Picts and Gaels, Galwegians and men of the Lothians. They were foot-soldiers with long spears and slashing swords, Lochaber axes and hunting daggers. Their shields were light and their armour scant, but their cause was good and their spirits high.

English soldier in armour and chain-mail.

Scottish soldier **below**

The English Advance

At last de Warenne and Cressingham were stirred to action. They led a powerful army from Berwick, north towards Stirling. At the head rode three hundred heavy cavalry, their rich surcoats and emblazoned shields bright in the sunlight. Behind marched the foot-soldiers and bowmen, ten thousand strong, well armed and well trained. With Dunbar and Irvine fresh in their minds, none had any reason to doubt their sure success. The very sight of this mighty column would bring the upstart rabble to their knees. Order would be restored in Edward's Scotland. Taxes would be collected once more.

The Battleground

A little over half a mile to the east of Stirling Castle the Forth makes one of its great horseshoe loops, swinging to the south and then curling tightly north again. It was on the upper reach of this bend, where it swings south, that the wooden bridge of Stirling spanned the wandering river. From its northern end a raised causeway led for a mile or so through the soft meadowlands held in the crook of the bend to the southern slope of Abbey Craig, a tree covered mound rising a hundred metres above the flatness of the carse. It

The River Forth at Stirling

was from here that William Wallace and Andrew Murray, their eyes narrowed against the brightness of early autumn, looked south to the bridge and out over the curling river and the plain beyond. It was early September and they had brought their forces down from the Ochil Hills to assemble under the cover of the trees on the southern side of the Craig. Now, united as one army against the intruder in their land, united in the cause of freedom, they waited. Wallace would have no dealings with the two Dominican Friars who brought John de Warenne, the Earl of Surrey's final request for surrender. The Scots would not yield. 'Tell your commander,' Wallace replied, 'we are here to defend ourselves and to free our kingdom. Let them come on, and we will meet them to their very beards.'

The Battle

And on they came. Two by two, the knights on their great chargers squeezed across the slender span. The bridge shook under the heavy hooves and the hollow rumble could be heard on Abbey Craig like distant thunder. Hugh de Cressingham claimed the honour of leading. He was impatient to be done with the troublesome rabble and anxious to spare his King's purse the strain of a long battle. Already and for the same reason, he had dismissed reinforcements under Henry Percy. Wallace watched as the great force spilled from the narrow neck of Stirling Bridge on to the carse in the loop of the river. He watched and waited as the English knights wrestled to bring their chargers into line on the soft footing of the meadowland to either side of the causeway. Almost half the force had made the crossing when the air was torn by the sudden blast of the Scots' war horn, the signal for which the freedom fighters had waited. With their war cry 'a Wallace' ringing over the plain, the Scottish spearmen raced down from Abbey Craig to split the English column at the north end of the bridge and to seal the narrow opening of the horseshoe. The trap was sprung. De Cressingham and his men would not escape. The battle was brief and brutal and the hated treasurer died by Scottish swords. His fat corpse was flayed and his skin cut in small pieces to be carried as tokens of freedom from all the oppression he and his kind had brought to Scotland.

With the bridge blocked by the dead and dying, Earl Warenne was powerless to help and could only watch the slaughter on the north bank. At last he ordered the bridge cut and made a swift retreat to Berwick, leaving his men to make the best of it. They soon found themselves bogged down in the salty marshes of Stirling plain and easy prey to the troops of those Scottish nobles whose forced loyalty to Edward had once more proved worthless. English losses on both sides of the Forth were huge.

Though the war was not yet won, the gallant Andrew Murray (who died that November of his terrible wounds) and William Wallace together showed that victory was possible; that an army of peasant soldiers could be inspired to defend their homeland against the foreign intruder. Behind these two young leaders they had won their place in the nation along with men of rank, Church and business.

The Hammer and the Lion

Wallace as Guardian

For ten months after his great victory at Stirling Bridge in September 1297, William Wallace was Guardian of the Kingdom of Scotland and commander of its armies. He governed in the name of John Balliol, still Edward's prisoner, and by consent of the Community of the Realm, which really meant all the King's subjects, common and noble—the whole nation. His ambition was to rid his homeland of English tyranny and see King John once more upon its throne. Apart from James the High Steward and the Earl of Lennox, whose combined troops had cut down the fleeing soldiers in the marshes south of Stirling Bridge, the Scottish nobles were too jealous or too proud to serve under a mere laird from Elderslie. They watched from the sidelines. And while Wallace fought for John Balliol he could expect little help from Robert Bruce who had his own ideas about who should be king.

The national army that Wallace commanded was made up of common folk and they had no choice but serve in it when called. While it was victorious no one could challenge his position as Guardian of Scotland and for a time it was successful. In the winter of 1297, Wallace marched into the north of England where plunder and booty would supply the soldiers' needs at a time of famine in Scotland. There the Scots ranged far and wide exacting revenge on other common folk like themselves. Without siege machinery they were unable to win castles where those who had planned and gained from Scotland's oppression remained secure behind towering walls: Berwick, Alnwick, Newcastle, Durham, Carlisle, and Edinburgh and Roxburgh too. Only Stirling Castle fell to Wallace and in the end wind-whipped snow and piercing frost drove the invaders home in early December.

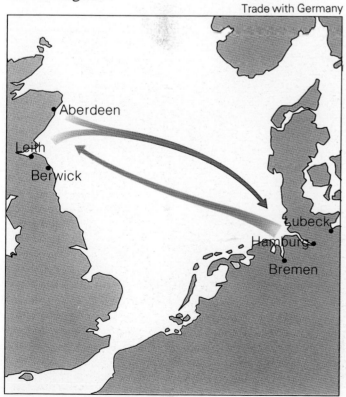

Letter from William Wallace and Andrew Murray to the merchants of Lübeck and Hamburg 1297, with **below** a translation

Trade

But Wallace did more than fight in his short rule. He opened the ports of Scotland to the merchants of Europe. Trade was vital if Scotland would survive as an independent kingdom, and he had been quick to write letters from Haddington to Lübeck and Hamburg, within a month of his victory at Stirling. He thanked the mayors of these German cities for their support and invited them to trade in safety once more with Scotland now that it was 'recovered by war from the power of the English'.

Trade with Germany

Andrew of Moray and William Wallace, leaders of the army of the kingdom of Scotland, and the community of the same kingdom, to the prudent and discreet men, their beloved friends the mayors and commons of Lübeck and of Hamburg, greeting and continual increase of sincere affection. It has been announced to us by trustworthy merchants of the said kingdom of Scotland that you, of your own grace and not out of regard for our deserts, are considerate, helpful and favourable in all causes and affairs touching us and our merchants; and therefore we are the more bound to you to give you our thanks and a worthy recompense whereto we willingly engage ourselves to you, beseeching you that you cause it to be proclaimed among your merchants that they may have a safe access to all ports of the kingdom of Scotland with their merchandise, because the kingdom of Scotland, thanks be to God, is recovered by war from the power of the English. Farewell.

We ask you, moreover, that you deign to promote the business of John Burnet and John Frere, our merchants, as you may wish us to promote the business of your merchants. Farewell.

Edward Plans Revenge

The same winter harshness that hurried the Scottish army homeward from England, made impossible any English campaign against the north. But in February 1298 word was received by John de Warenne that Edward, Hammer of the Scots, was returning from Flanders to deal with the rebels personally. No action would be taken until then. In March, Edward's preparations began. He set his headquarters at York and gathered to his standard a powerful army with which to crush all resistance north of the border.

The Battle of Falkirk

In Linlithgow, the dawn stillness of Tuesday 22nd July was shattered as Edward's great army pressed through the town to close with the long searched for enemy. Clearly lit by the morning sun the Scots were seen making what preparations they could to withstand the crushing charges of the most feared cavalry in Europe. Wallace's task now was to inspire his men with courage in the face of impossible odds, to stand fast against the might of these iron men on their iron horses.

At Falkirk there was no looping river, no narrow bridge, no Abbey Craig. Here the best the Scots could do was to stand and kneel in tightly packed circles with their spears angled and grounded, thrusting out and up like the steel barbs of some monstrous hedgehog. There were more than a thousand men in each of Wallace's four human fortresses. To trouble the English cavalry angled stakes were driven into the ground round each of these great schiltrons, and roped together. What bowmen he had Wallace placed in the spaces between the four schiltrons, and to the rear the small cavalry commanded by those nobles who had joined him. It was not a strong position but the foot-soldiers were resolute. Wallace knew the situation was desperate and his final words to his men before the battle were, 'I have brought you to the ring, now dance if you can'.

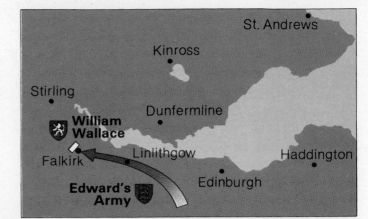

Map of battle site today

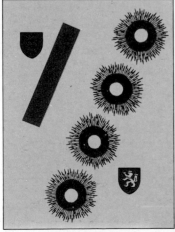

Plan of schiltron formation

The whole battle hung on the courage of Wallace's peasant soldiers. Each man braced himself to receive the full weight of the first charge. The blare of the horn followed by the growing thunder of the great horses and the charging hedge of levelled lances tested to the very limit each man's courage. That first charge rode down the Scottish archers to a man and scattered their cavalry in fleeing panic. The schiltrons held. Again and again, came the great shock waves of the mighty horsemen and still the rings of steel were not broken. But then the bowmen came within range and raised their long bows skywards. Under the killing rain, gaps opened in the defiant schiltrons which could not be filled. The dour struggle became a rout, the long drawn out battle was suddenly a slaughter and Edward had his revenge.

Wallace escaped with his life but not his guardianship. He never again led his country in peace or war but he had stirred a spirit of national pride that outlived defeat and stiffened his countrymen's will to resist the ambitious Kings of England.

After the Battle

Victory gave Edward little. He pushed on to Stirling to find it in ruins and took more revenge by burning St Andrews. When he turned south for home he left behind a land in which no Englishman was safe unless within the walls of a garrisoned castle. The Scots had learned to avoid pitched battles and for five years after the Battle of Falkirk, Scotland was never properly under the power of England. Always there were risings and attacks by the freedom fighters led now by the nobles who took over as Guardians after Wallace gave up control.

Bruce Changes Sides

In 1302, Robert Bruce who had fought steadily though not always successfully against England swore loyalty once more to Edward. He may have done so because of his own claim to the Scottish throne hoping that Edward would uphold it or simply because he could not support those who wanted to put the crown once more on the head of John Balliol. In any case he fought with no heart in the English cause and was never really trusted by Edward.

Roslin

Towards the end of the same year a powerful body of knights and mounted spearmen was sent north to test Scottish defences particularly to the west of Edinburgh, where the Forth might be crossed. Edward was already planning his next campaign against the north and had summoned his host to assemble in May 1303. By February 24th these advance brigades were approaching Roslin only seven miles south of the capital. Unknown to their leader Sir John Segrave, a strong force of Scots astride their shaggy ponies were closing fast from Biggar, only twenty-five miles to the south-west. Led by the Red Comyn and Simon Fraser, they rode under cover of darkness and struck at first light. The English column was taken by surprise and routed. Edward had now a double reason for his new campaign. Roslin would not be forgotten.

Late 13th century woodcut of Edward I

Late 16th century illustration
of Bruce and his first wife
Isabelle of Mar

Scotland Subdued

Once more the King of England led his mighty war machine against the 'rebel' Scots. It surged forward from Roxburgh on 30th May 1303, like some avenging dragon, burning and wasting the land, swallowing strongholds and castles for what nourishment they could provide. Even the River Forth was no barrier. Sectional bridges built in Norfolk were carried by sea to span the river. By 10th June, Perth had fallen and by September the Royal Standard of England was shown in Kinloss on the Moray Firth before Edward turned south again to Dunfermline where he made his head-quarters until the Spring of 1304. He received the usual surrenders and oaths of loyalty from the nobility. Scotland was once more subdued.

Though he gave fair and prudent terms to the defeated Scots, Edward's vengeance was not yet satisfied. Two things remained to taunt him. Above the battlements of Stirling Castle there still fluttered defiantly the proud and fierce emblem of Scotland, the Lion Rampant. He would not rest until it was torn down. Worse still, Sir William Wallace though no longer the leader was still active against him. He could not rest until this 'chief of brigands' was brought on his knees before him.

Bridging the Forth

Preparation for the siege of Stirling

From St Andrews fast horses made good speed to Chester bringing to the bishop the King's greetings and orders to see that supplies and stores were safely hastened to Stirling for his use there. They rode to York for loads of quick sulphur, cotton thread and saltpetre, also arrows well feathered and iron tipped. By 12th April he was at Kinghorn sending word to his son, the Prince Edward of Caernarvon, that lead was to be stripped from church roofs in Perth and Dunblane and elsewhere to make weights for his siege machines. He warned that none should be taken that protected the altar. And from Inverkeithing on 16th April he was issuing final instructions about the great engine of Inverkip and other devices for hurling stones and deadly Greek Fire. His preparations made, King Edward settled down before the great fortress on Stirling rock and on 21st April 1304 began the long siege. In a well placed house in the town a special window was made so that his young queen and her ladies could watch in comfort.

The Assault

At once Edward showed he was in no mood for the kind of chivalry usually shown to defenders in those days. Sir William Oliphant, the garrison commander, asked that a message should be sent to Sir John de Soules. It was Sir John who had first entrusted the castle to his keeping and he wanted to know if he should now surrender it. Edward refused. If Sir William could not have this advice then he would resist in the name of the Lion, which meant King of Scotland. The small garrison bent stubbornly to the bold defence of the castle without hope of relief. In the end, after three long months of pounding siege, it was hunger and hopelessness that forced the garrison to submit on 20th July 1304. In an act of bitter cruelty, Edward rejected their unconditional surrender until, for one further and needless day, they were battered in their broken castle by the latest of his engines of destruction—the Warwolf. This final assault ended, the garrison escaped a terrible execution only by begging for mercy on their knees before the English King and even then only because others who were with Edward pleaded for them. All fifty were sent to prisons in England.

With the fall of Stirling Castle, Edward believed that there was no longer any kingdom of the Scots. Now all that remained for him to do was to complete his plans for their government which he had begun at St Andrews, before the siege. This he would do in his parliament at Westminster in September 1305 when ten Scots would join with twenty-one Englishmen in drawing up the final settlement.

Siege Weapons

Round the ramparts Edward's engineers and carpenters built a great battery of the biggest and best engines of war ever constructed. Each had its own level standing, cut in the sloping ground, and a shield of stout wooden posts to give protection from the defenders' arrows and missiles. Day after day, as spring became summer, the long throwing arms of the mighty trebuchets hurled massive boulders over the fortress walls while smaller ballista whipped deadlier fireballs against anything that would burn. Men and horses strained at the great belfry tower with which to find a way over the walls while teams with heavy rams toiled to smash their way in.

Stirling Castle today

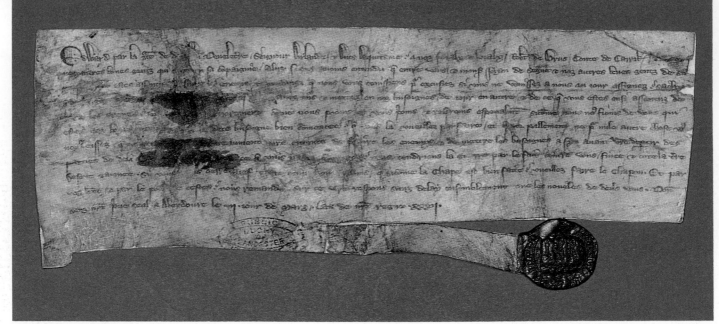

Letter from Edward I to Robert Bruce who was fighting on the side of the English in 1304

The Seal of Edward I

The Settlement

And it was a fair settlement they agreed that autumn, giving little but taking away less. In Edward's 'Ordinances for the Government of the Land of Scotland' the Scottish people would have the same laws, customs and freedoms as they enjoyed under King Alexander III, but, of course, they would have only Edward for their lord. This time it was a light 'hammer' which forged what was meant to be a long and peaceful English rule in Scotland. Edward knew he could not hold the Scottish people by force for ever. He had been mild and fair in his terms and inflicted few punishments for all their offences.

Wallace Captured

Shortly after the general surrender in February of 1304, Edward issued the proclamation, 'Know that it is not our will that you hold out any word of peace to either him or to any of his company . . .' He meant Wallace. From that day forth, the Scottish hero was hunted until at last he was seized on the third day of August somewhere in the Glasgow area. Twenty days later in Westminster Hall he was tried without jury and condemned without defence. That same day he was dragged to Smithfield, and brutally executed in public for treason. At no time did he admit any loyalty to

Edward but had always fought for the rightful King of Scotland. By making Wallace suffer the shameful death of a traitor Edward hoped to frighten anyone who might think to copy his example. In fact he succeeded only in making sure that the example would never be forgotten. The burning and killing, the famine and misery would slowly fade from memory, but Wallace and his spirit would be remembered forever. There would be no easy bending to the rule of England's King.

Worksection

The Freedom Fighters
Understand Your Work

Edward and Scotland
1 What was it that Edward feared Scotland would do?
2 How might this affect his own plans?
3 What does the old rhyme mean,
  'If that you will France win,
  Then with Scotland first begin.'?
4 In 1296, did Edward believe he had put down the Scots?
5 What mistakes had he made?
6 Whose name was missing from the pages of the Ragman Roll?
7 Who held Scotland for King Edward?
8 Why was he a bad choice for the post?

William Wallace
1 What did Wallace do in May 1297 which began the fight for freedom?
2 What had caused him to do this?
3 Which English official ran the day to day affairs of Scotland?
4 What was he called, by the Scots?
5 Who declared William Wallace to be an outlaw?
6 How did Wallace show what he thought of this man and his power?
7 Who else were leading uprisings in Scotland at this time?
8 Where were these other uprisings?

Edward Strikes Back
1 Why did Edward strike at the uprising of the nobles?
2 What made the English army much too strong for the Scots?
3 How did the Scottish leaders gain some advantage after refusing to fight?
4 Who was Andrew Murray leading and where was he fighting?
5 Where did Murray and Wallace meet for the first time?
6 How were their men armed and armoured?
7 What size of force did Edward send against the Scots?
8 Find on a map of Scotland the place where the two armies met.

The Battle of Stirling Bridge
1 Describe the battleground where Wallace and Murray faced the English.
2 Where had the Scots gathered and how did they keep out of sight of the enemy?
3 What first shows that John de Warenne, Earl of Surrey, believed the Scots would be quick to surrender?
4 Who led the English force across Stirling Bridge?
5 What shows that he too thought victory was certain and easy?
6 What was the signal for the Scots advance?
7 How were the English soldiers trapped?
8 What was surprising about the fact that the Scots army had won?

The Hammer and the Lion

Wallace as Guardian
1 What position did William Wallace hold in Scotland after the Battle of Stirling Bridge in 1297?
2 How do you know that Wallace did not think of himself as King?
3 What difficulty did Wallace suffer because he was not a noble?
4 Why did the Scots army fail to take the castles which sheltered their enemies?
5 How did Wallace try to improve Scotland's trade during his rule?
6 What delayed Edward's campaign to overthrow Wallace?
7 When did he finally bring Wallace to battle?
8 Find on your map the area where the battle took place.

The Battle of Falkirk
1 How did the battleground at Falkirk differ from the conditions at Stirling Bridge?
2 How did Wallace arrange his men?
3 What did he do to upset the English chargers?
4 What did Wallace mean, when he said to his men – 'I have brought you to the ring, now dance if you can.'?
5 What effect had the first of the English charges on the Scottish army?
6 What was a schiltron?
7 How were the schiltrons weakened so that they could be broken by the cavalry?
8 What effect had the defeat at Falkirk on Wallace?
9 What effect did it have on the Scottish people?

After the Battle
1 Edward had crushed Wallace's army at Falkirk. Did this victory give him control of Scotland?
2 How did the Scots carry on the resistance?
3 How did Edward test the Scottish defences on the River Forth near Edinburgh?
4 What happened to his advance brigade at Roslin?
5 How did the English army cross the Forth in the Spring Campaign of 1303?
6 On this occasion Edward was fair in his treatment of the defeated Scots. What two things still angered him?

The Siege of Stirling Castle
1 From what places were Edward's supplies and weapons brought?
2 What do you think the sulphur, cotton thread and saltpetre were required for?
3 How was lead obtained and from where?
4 How were the great siege weapons set up on ground that sloped?
5 What types of machines did Edward use?
6 What special arrangements were made for the comfort of the English Queen and her ladies?
7 In the end what caused the garrison to surrender?
8 What act of needless cruelty did King Edward commit against the tiny garrison?

The Settlement

1 What did King Edward believe had happened because Stirling Castle had fallen?
2 How did he make arrangements for the government of Scotland?
3 What had the English King learned about keeping the Scots under his control?
4 Where and when was Wallace finally captured?
5 What was unusual about Wallace's trial?
6 What did the English King hope to do by treating Wallace so harshly?
7 What, in fact, was the result of this harshness?

Use Your Imagination

1 What do you think were the main differences between the Scottish and the English armies?
2 Did any of these differences give the Scots a better chance of winning?
3 Do you think it would be possible for Scots foot soldiers to seriously wound an armoured knight? How would they do this?
4 How do you suppose the English army used its various types of soldier in battle?
5 What steps could you take to defend yourself against the cavalry and the archers?
6 Can you think of any reasons why it might be better to capture rather than harm knights of the opposing army?
7 Did this give them an advantage in war when compared with the common soldiers? Do you feel this was fair? Do you think it is still true today?
8 Why do you suppose John de Warenne cut Stirling Bridge before fleeing from the battle?
9 Wallace's and Murray's plan at Stirling Bridge was simple enough. Why do you suppose the English commanders walked into the trap?
10 Do you think it was wise of Wallace to face the English army at Falkirk? Why do you suppose he did so?
11 What tactics could Wallace have used against an army away from home, on wild Scottish countryside?
12 Why do you think King Edward was so anxious to win back Stirling Castle. Why do you suppose he was so brutal in his treatment of the brave garrison?
13 What, in your opinion, has made Wallace such a well loved figure in Scottish history?
14 Do you think it was just and wise to declare William Wallace a traitor?

Further Work

1 Try to arrange a visit to the Wallace Memorial on Abbey Craig at Stirling. From its height you will see the Forth snaking across the carse and you will learn a good deal about William Wallace.

2 It was only after many months of bitter fighting that the two great freedom fighters William Wallace and Andrew Murray met face to face for the very first time. No doubt what they had heard of each other's success, had given them courage, but now in the Ochil Hills they could join forces. Try to imagine this historic meeting and the feelings of the men. Be a reporter and write an account of the great moment.

3 The meeting of Wallace and Murray would make a very dramatic picture. You could paint it all in one colour in the following way:
First decide on a strong dark dramatic colour, thick and solid. Then make a light tone of this colour by mixing it with white paint.
Use this light tone to make your background by carefully covering your whole paper with a storm of windswept swirls and dots.
When this is dry take the thick strong tone of the same colour and paint the sloping rough ground line.

either this way or. .

. . this way

With the same thick colour, paint silhouettes of the two heroic knights at their first meeting. Finish off with foreground rocks, grass, bushes etc. Use the same strong thick paint.
Prepare a name caption and mount your picture for display.

4 At dawn on Tuesday, July 22nd 1298, in the town of Linlithgow, the stillness was shattered by the approaching din of Edward's army. Try to imagine that you were there, wakened by the noise, amazed and frightened by the sight. Write a description of what you saw, heard, felt and thought

5 How long is an army? You could work out the length of a column of ten thousand men marching five abreast by measuring the length of a column of ten of your classmates and multiplying your answer.
Soldiers march at about 5 kilometres per hour. Can you work out how long the column would take to pass you if you were standing waiting to cross the road? Are there other things you can work out? Discuss it in your group and make up a list of interesting facts about a marching army.

A King without a Kingdom

Bruce Claims the Throne

By the year 1305, there was no King in Scotland, no Lion Rampant and no Wallace. Instead, all the major castles were in Edward's hands and a new system of English government had been set up. For more than half a year it must have seemed that all was well. Then the news reached Edward. On the 25th March 1306, exactly ten years after Edward's first invasion of the north, Robert Bruce crowned himself King of Scotland at Scone. It had all begun again.

Death of the Red Comyn

In fact it had begun six weeks earlier when the Red Comyn and Robert Bruce met in Greyfriars Kirk in Dumfries, possibly to discuss plans for revolution. The men were bitter rivals and violent argument broke out between them. Bruce struck down Comyn with his dagger and his companions finished the business leaving the dying man on the altar steps. Murder, sacrilege, treason—all these things Robert Bruce was guilty of. His life was forfeit. His only hope lay in the plans for revol-

ution he had already made. These he put into action at once. In the weeks that followed Bruce and a growing band of followers seized castles and towns and began raising his army. With desperate haste he urged the rebellion across the land, arriving at Scone with sixty armed men. There he was proclaimed King of Scotland in ancient and solemn ceremony. This time the way to freedom would be led by a King.

Already Edward's long shadow crept menacingly over the land. He was now an elderly man whose patience and nature had grown brittle with his ageing bones. In a fury of revenge he moved against Bruce and his followers. The murderers of the Red Comyn would suffer as Wallace had suffered. In blood and fire the traitor 'King Hob' would be brought down. That Robert Bruce had a proper claim to the throne of the kingdom of the Scots meant nothing to Edward who did not accept that there was any such kingdom.

Battle of Methven

Aymer de Valence, Earl of Pembroke was chosen to be Edward's special commander in Scotland. Flying the terrible dragon banner to declare that no mercy would be shown, he marched against the rebels slaying all who resisted his King's will, and laying waste their lands with fire and sword. Those had been his orders. On Sunday 19th June at Methven to the west of Perth, he surprised and routed Bruce and his men. Less than three months from the day he had taken the throne at Scone, King Robert was in flight for his life through a land where the enemy had left him no place of refuge. By cunning and secret help he wriggled through the tight net cast round him by the English commander and disappeared into the west and the isles beyond. Edward urged his men to search out the King in hiding and bring him to justice. The country was scoured but not the slightest trace could be found. Even now no one is sure where Bruce spent those lost months.

Methven castle

The Tomb of Aymer de Valence in Westminster Abbey

Coat of Arms of Aymer de Valence

Night Raid on Turnberry Castle

In the mist and winter darkness of a February night in 1307, shadowy craft, guided to Turnberry Point by the glowing signal of a secret beacon, slid quietly on to the beach below the Castle. Armed men left the boats and moved swiftly and silently inland. They were led by two men. One was the tall slim figure of the Black Douglas, the other was Robert Bruce. The plan that night was to seize by surprise attack the coastal stronghold of Turnberry Castle, but already something was wrong. The signal fire which should have beckoned them only to a safe landing had been lit in error or even as a trap. English patrols were everywhere. The castle could not be stormed. Instead, Bruce and his men came out of the night to fall upon the resting soldiers of Sir Henry Percy's garrison in their hutted camp outside the castle walls. Many of the garrison died in that attack. The raiders made off with ample plunder and good English horses to their hideout in the hills of Carrick. It was there that Bruce learned that three of his brothers had been executed and his wife, daughter and two sisters were in harsh imprisonment, all on the order of Edward, King of England. In the high ground of his native Carrick he had time to count the cost of his bid for kingship.

Turnberry castle

Edward Marches North

Angered by his commander's failure to put down the rebel Scots, Edward once more called to the field the mighty army of England and marched north. His spirit was as strong and as fierce as it had ever been but his body at last proved too frail. On the 7th July 1307, just three miles from the border, the Hammer of the Scots died. Though his son, Edward of Carnarvon, had his father's name and wore his father's crown, he took little delight in the hard harsh life of a soldier king. He led the great host forward as far as Cumnock in Ayrshire then turned south again without engaging Bruce in battle.

Civil War in Scotland

With the English army out of the way, with Aymer de Valance and his knights recalled to England by Edward II, Bruce was now free to wage a brief and bitter civil war on the supporters of Comyn and Balliol. First, he turned on Galloway with such force that some of his enemies at once fled to England while those who remained paid heavily for a short truce. Then he marched north into the highlands where John Comyn whose father Bruce had slain in Greyfriars Church, held out against him in the Earldom of Buchan. In November, Bruce's army swept through the Great Glen taking the castles of Inverlochy, Urquhart and Inverness.

Sites in Civil War

Elgin Castle proved too stubborn and Bruce left it for another day. Now he moved south into Buchan, the heart of Comyn country. The whole north-east of Scotland was within his grasp as he marched boldly for Inverurie, when all the hardship and strain he had endured over many months finally caught up with the exhausted King. Weakness and sickness overcame his strength and he collapsed. His army halted some way north and to the west of Inverurie and those who had little taste for following a dying leader deserted his standard. With fewer than a thousand faithful men he rested at Slioch in the valley of the Deveron, two miles south-east of Huntly.

Huntly Castle

Winter of 1307

By Christmas day there was snow on the ground and the river ran cold and grey between its white banks. Among the leafless trees Bruce's weary men huddled against the winter with little comfort and less food. News of the King's dwindling strength brought John Comyn, Earl of Buchan, in force against them. But it was a feeble encounter in which, for a day or two, aimless arrows fell amongst the trees and in the snow. Sure that he could rout his weakened and leaderless force the Earl withdrew to gather more men for what would be a final assault. He returned on Hogmanay confident of victory only to be met by such a bold show of strength led by the King's brother, Sir Edward Bruce, that the surprised Earl did not dare attack. It was to prove a serious mistake.

The Herschip of Buchan

As King Robert's strength returned, so did the strength of his army. By May 1308, more castles had fallen, and again he closed on the Earl of Buchan at Inverurie. The battle should have taken place on the rising ground by Old Meldrum looking over the place where the River Ury flows into the Don. Here the Earl awaited the arrival of the ailing King and his weary army. But there was no battle. The mere sight of Bruce astride his horse at the head of the approaching column was enough. As the King's spearmen bore down on the men of Buchan they retreated and then fled. The king laid waste the whole earldom with such violence that those terrible days were forever remembered as the 'Herschip of Buchan.'

Loch Awe and the Pass of Brander from Ben Cruachen, Argyll

The MacDougalls

Turning then to the south-west, Bruce marched on Argyll where the Clan MacDougall, led by John of Lorne, still resisted. He came by Dalmally to the narrow pass of Brander where the track was squeezed for seven miles between the edge of Loch Awe and the sheer south face of the misty Ben Cruachan. Hidden on the mountain's treacherous slopes the MacDougalls lay in wait for Bruce. As his army moved through the pass, the hillside watchers prepared, on a signal, to hurl down an avalanche of boulders upon the King's men, killing some, trapping all as easy prey for the bowmen of Lorne. But the signal that came was from higher on Cruachan's great shoulder and to another body of soldiers. At once, the archers of the Black Douglas thumbed their bowstrings, releasing a hail of arrows down among John of Lorne's men. King Robert had been wary of just such an ambush and had sent James Douglas and his highlanders scrambling over the high ground while the main army marched through the pass. Now it was the MacDougalls who found themselves in the trap with Douglas charging down on them and Bruce advancing from below. They and their leader, who had remained in his galley on Loch Awe, fled in panic. Argyll submitted to the new King.

The English Castles

Before the end of that year the Scottish King had put down all who had opposed him. The civil war was won. He must now win back the strongholds still held in the name of Edward II by English garrisons—Perth, Edinburgh, Roxburgh, Linlithgow, Direlton, Dunbar, Stirling, Berwick and more. And one by one they fell, but not to the pounding of ballista and battering ram or the long hungry months of close siege. Rather, it was by stealth and skill. Bruce and his young captains led their men on daring raids under cover of darkness, silently and swiftly crossing the moat, then scaling the high walls by grappling hook and rope ladder.

Perth, Roxburgh & Edinburgh

When Perth proved too strong behind its great walls and towers of stone, its wide moat and the River Tay, Bruce pretended to lift the siege and withdraw. Within a week and by dead of night he returned. Shoulder deep in the icy blackness of the moat he led his men across to the walls. Behind such a leader neither high walls nor armed garrison could resist them. A year later on a night in February, James Douglas cloaked his men in black and approached unseen to scale the walls of Roxburgh Castle. Within a month and in the darkness, Thomas Randolph with thirty men climbed the sheer face of Castle Rock in Edinburgh to admit the main force through the East Port and seize the great fortress.

Edward Bruce's Bargain

For seven long years Bruce had fought with cunning, making strength of his army's weaknesses and turning English advantages to handicaps. The great strength and weight of the English army, so feared in battle, made it slow of movement and in constant need of supplies. Bruce developed a force that was quick and mobile, and based it far from Edward's supply centres. The Scots were raiders, fast and sudden, travelling on light horses with the least amount of equipment and food. Whenever possible they cut the English lines of supply, always refusing pitched battle. It was with these tactics that King Robert won back all the most important castles except Stirling and

it had been under close siege for some time. It was Sir Edward Bruce who commanded the siege and who made the bargain which put at risk all his brother the King had won. Sir Edward had arranged with Sir Philip Mowbray, commander of the castle, that it would be surrendered if it was not relieved by King Edward II before Midsummer Day 1314. Of course, the King of England was bound by honour to come, and battle would then be joined.

Portrait of Robert Bruce (1274–1329) by Jamesone

Bannockburn

In the bright sunshine of a June afternoon, the commander-in-chief checked yet again his forward positions. He was satisfied. His soldiers, four divisions of them, were well placed and screened by the trees on the rising ground of New Park Forest, two miles south of Stirling. Any cavalry charge launched against them would be uphill and there was sufficient cover to make arrows less deadly. In addition to these natural defences, a network of pits had been dug and lightly covered, and a great many four pointed iron calthrops lay hidden amongst the long marsh grasses. Round all of this, a narrow burn wriggled its course down through the Park and on to join the River Forth. It was called the Bannock.

Beyond the burn and against the brightness the commander could see a forest of swaying banners and lances thrusting upwards from rank upon rank of advancing knights on great chargers, the hammerhead of a mighty host. They were much nearer now and he could make out the colours of their emblazoned surcoats against the blackness of the armour. Those further back were still obscured in the rising dust cloud that hung over the long column. It was a time to be steadfast.

Apart from the gold circlet crown on his plain helmet he might have been taken for any field commander—but this was Robert Bruce, King of Scotland. It was the 23rd June 1314, and the battle of Bannockburn was about to commence.

In his four divisions Bruce had about 6,000 battle hardened troops including a light cavalry of some five hundred and a few score archers from Ettrick Forest. He marched them from Torwood to their battle positions on Saturday, 22nd June where they now waited.

On the other side of the burn a powerful English army was advancing on the Scottish lines. Edward had summoned to his standard almost three thousand heavy cavalry and more than seventeen thousand spearmen and archers. In addition, there was a baggage train of two hundred wagons dragged by teams of oxen. The column, more than two miles in length, was led by knights in their dark armour and brightly coloured shields and surcoats, all mounted on powerful chargers which were lightly armoured and draped in rich flowing trappers to entangle spears and swords. Edward II, King of England, had come at last to claim his inheritance and to crush 'Robert de Brus who calls himself King of Scotland'.

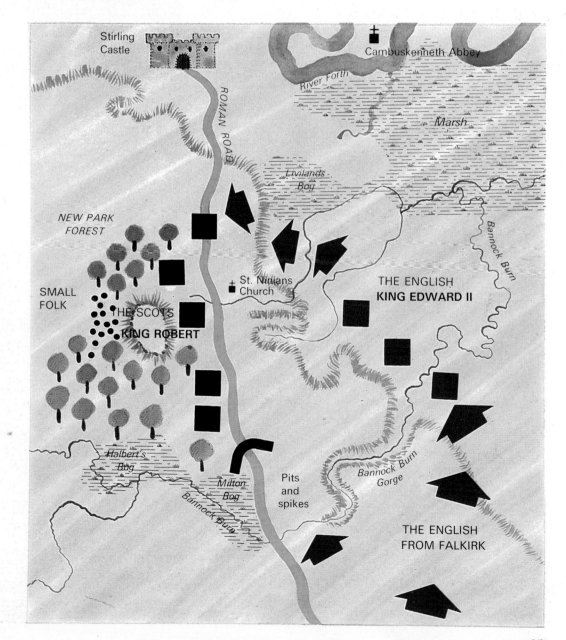

As the van of the huge force approached the Scottish position the most forward of Bruce's men withdrew to the cover of the woodland. One amongst the English host noted the small gold coronet worn by the Scottish King. Levelling his pennoned lance and spurring his horse, Sir Henry de Bohun tilted at the unprepared Scot. A second from impact Robert Bruce reined his pony sharply and suddenly to one side and, rising in his saddle, struck a fatal blow down through the charging knight's helmet. The very first encounter of the day was over and the heavily armed and armoured had been overpowered by the lighter and more agile. The lesson was learned by the Scots and their spirits rose.

In good heart they braced themselves against the faceless iron men whose lowered lance points now surged towards them. Suddenly the English Cavalry was amongst the pits and spikes. Horses stumbled and reared and the charge was broken. The Scots, seeing the confusion, pressed forward down the sloping ground.

The cavalry retired across the burn and the second encounter of the day had gone well for the small Scottish army. Foot soldiers had again prevailed against horse. A third encounter was to take place that day. Earlier, Edward had dispatched a force of some five hundred knights under Sir Robert Clifford and Sir Henry Beaumont on a flanking movement. This cavalry force made swift and secret passage along The Way at the edge of the Carse of Stirling, the low ground to the eastern side of the Scottish lines. Almost too late their progress was observed, and seeing the danger Bruce ordered Thomas Randolph to intercept.

Randolph's schiltron moved down the slope and was at once spotted by Clifford. Cunningly he drew his cavalry back encouraging the Scots to press forward clear of the high ground which was broken and unsuited to horse. On and on came Randolph's men in open formation. Suddenly and without warning the English lance points dropped level and the massive charge thundered forward. With equal suddenness the open formation of the Scots, so frail before the weight of the English armour, snapped shut to form an unbreakable ring of barbed steel. Despite all the fury of the English attack the schiltron held. Desperately, the knights hurled lances and maces as they circled the rock steady spears. When Randolph counter attacked, the English were driven from the field. Three times Edward's mighty host had thrust and three times Bruce's men had parried. The sun was low now and the engagement was broken off for the night.

Monday was hot again and the Scots rose early for prayers and to renew the battle at first light. But all was different now. During the late evening and throughout the night the English army had been moving into the marshy wetness of the Carse. Why Edward made the decision to order his great army into that terrible position is not known. Perhaps he was confident that a force as small as the Scottish army would never risk leaving the security of the high ground to attempt a full scale advance. Indeed he may have felt attack so unlikely that he thought it quite safe to move into the Carse in order that his thirsty men and animals might drink. Whatever the explanation the move would prove to be a terrible misjudgment. Edward's noble army was now trapped on an island of marsh veined with tiny streams and pools, each a hazard to his mighty cavalry. If the King of Scotland would have his kingdom—now was the day.

The sun was climbing directly behind the crowded English lines when Bruce's men moved down off the high ground and tramped steadily forward across the Carse. The advance was led by Sir Edward Bruce, supported on his left by Thomas Randolph's division and that of James Douglas with the King's men closely behind. The movements of the four divisions were clearly lit in morning brightness. To King Edward the sight was astonishing. It was simply not possible that such a puny army would commit itself to attack. When the Scots stooped and knelt some hundreds of yards from the English line, Edward felt sure they were in the act of seeking his mercy. Those who looked more carefully, saw that Bruce's divisions were checking and tightening their schiltron formations. In good discipline the men knelt and crouched with spears angled and grounded against any sudden charge of the English heavy armour. At last the King of England was persuaded that the Scots meant to fight and his trumpets sounded.

The call to advance caught some of the knights unprepared and the first charge was ragged and uncertain. The horses had difficulty in the heavy uneven ground and Edward Bruce's schiltrons held. Randolph and Douglas closed in support and the Scottish line did not falter. The cavalry, now unable to regroup properly, fell back before the spear hedge that bore down on them. The Scottish line spanned the gap between the Bannock and the Pelstream. The English soldiers could deploy to neither flank and their spearmen were unable to fight back, hemmed in as they were behind the cavalry. Crushed at the rear, the Welsh archers could do little to help their comrades. Arrows shot high fell more often than not on their own van and seldom troubled the advancing Scots.

The plight of the English soldiers was desperate but they fought on with dogged courage and determination. Relief was won for a short period, when a company or two of archers were successfully deployed north of the Scottish line and brought their fire to bear on the densely packed flank of Douglas's division. Seeing the danger, Bruce signalled to Sir Robert Keith who was stationed with his light cavalry on the high ground. Under the flowing red, yellow and white banner of the Earl Marshal, the Scottish light horse plunged down the sloping ground and across the Carse to scatter the bowmen. For the first and only time horse had the better of it in an engagement.

With the passing of this brief recovery the English staggered back before the Scottish schiltrons. Sensing that the crisis was near, Bruce threw in his reserve division of Highlanders to press home the advantage. If the King of Scotland would have his kingdom, now was the hour.

All four divisions were in line, a great arc of mounting pressure bearing down remorselessly upon the knights and upon the spearmen beyond. The ten battalions of Edward's army were now compressed into one helpless mass of men and horses. At last, and only after the most stubborn and gallant resistance the English foot faltered. Soldiers in the rearmost ranks broke formation and began to flee across the Bannock.

The King of England seeing that the day was lost, was persuaded to leave the field. A body of several hundred knights closed about his person and cut their way through the Scottish line to escape along the banks of the River Forth towards Stirling Castle. The sight of the Royal Standard leaving the field, signalled the end of the beleaguered army's hard fought and honourable struggle. English soldiers were pursued in ever direction, many to drown in the waters of the Forth while others were forced into the muddy gorge of the Bannock in the rising tide. For his own security Edward himself was refused entry to the castle, where, under the terms of the bargain with Sir Edward Bruce, he would have become a Scottish captive the following day. With James Douglas in close pursuit he managed to reach Dunbar, from where he was taken by small boat to the safety of Berwick and the south. The might of England had been subdued in formal battle. The King of Scotland had his kingdom.

Worksection

A King without a Kingdom
Understand Your Work

Bruce

1 What state was Scotland in by the year 1305?
2 What happened which changed all this?
3 How did the meeting between the Red Comyn and Robert Bruce in Greyfriars Church, Dumfries end?
4 In the weeks that followed how did Bruce attempt to save himself?
5 How did Edward behave when Bruce crowned himself King of Scotland?
6 Why did Edward ignore Bruce's claim to the Scottish throne?
7 What huge task lay ahead for the new King?
8 How did Bruce plan to fight the mighty armies of England?

The First Blow

1 In what area did Bruce begin his fight back?
2 Where did he first come face to face with a strong English force?
3 How did the Scots prepare for the battle?
4 What did the English commander think was going to be the result of the battle?
5 Why did the famed English cavalry fail to trouble the Scots?
6 How did the Scots press home their advantage?
7 Where did Aymer de Valance seek safety?
8 Why was this an important victory for Bruce?

Civil War

1 What caused the English King not to avenge the defeat at Loudoun Hill?
2 Because the English did not attack, Bruce had time to settle his own troubles at home. What were these?
3 How did Bruce set about bringing the whole kingdom under his rule?
4 Where and why did he almost fail?
5 What was the Herschip of Buchan?
6 Where did Bruce go after defeating John Comyn, Earl of Buchan?
7 Where was he almost ambushed?
8 How did the King avoid the trap and defeat the Clan MacDougall?

Taking The Castles

1 What castles did Bruce now recover from the English?
2 How did his methods differ from Edward I's siege of Stirling Castle?
3 How did Bruce take Perth Castle despite its great strength?
4 What method did James Douglas employ to take Roxburgh Castle?
5 How did Thomas Randolph surprise the garrison at Edinburgh Castle?

6 How did Bruce fight his campaign against an enemy with a better, stronger army?
7 What advantage did the Scots King have?
8 What was the bargain his brother made that caused the King to change tactics and face the English in pitched battle?

Bannockburn

1 How was the Scottish army divided at Bannockburn?
2 Where were the soldiers positioned?
3 What advantage and protection did this give them?
4 Who led the English Army?
5 How was it made up?
6 What purpose did the trappers serve which were draped around the Knights' chargers?
7 What preparations had the Scottish King made to strengthen his position in New Park Forest?
8 What did the Scots do as they saw the might of England advance towards them?

The Battle

1 Who was the first casualty in the Battle of Bannockburn?
2 What caused the first English cavalry charge to fail?
3 How did Edward attempt to get past the Scots army and relieve the castle without battle?
4 How did Thomas Randolph's men stop the English knights?
5 What mistake did King Edward II make after the first day?
6 Why did Edward think the Scots were seeking mercy?
7 Why did the English Cavalry fail on the second day?
8 What prevented the Welsh bowmen bringing their fire to bear on the Scottish ranks?
9 How did King Robert break the English resistance?
10 Why was Edward II refused entry to Stirling Castle?
11 How did he finally make his escape?

Use Your Imagination

1 Do you think Robert Bruce planned to kill the Red Comyn?

2 What lessons do you think Robert Bruce learned from the Battle of Falkirk?

3 To be the 'ghost' army that Bruce needed, what training and skills would his soldiers require?

4 Why do you suppose Bruce decided to face Aymer de Valance at Loudoun Hill?

5 What made it important that the new King defeated his enemies at home as quickly as possible?

6 Why did Bruce not use massive siege weapons or starve out garrisons to win back the castles?

7 The bargain made by Edward Bruce with the Commander of Stirling Castle angered King Robert. Why do you think this was so?

8 Robert Bruce had his army arranged in New Park Forest just as though they had been marched from Torwood and then turned about to face the south from where the enemy would approach. The rearguard was now the front line. Can you think of any reason why the King may have done this?

9 Why do you think a calthrop has four points?

10 Why do you suppose Sir Henry de Bohun attempted to kill King Robert?

11 What made Edward so sure the Scots would not attack?

12 For what purpose do you think the Scots cavalry had been kept on the high ground away from the fighting?

Further Work

1 In the winter darkness of a February night in 1306, shadowy craft, guided to Turnberry Point by the red glow of a secret beacon, slid noiselessly towards the empty beach. Robert Bruce had come home to claim his kingdom . . .

Imagine that you are in one of the little boats. You can barely see the other boats in the darkness but you can just hear the occasional sounds as you draw nearer to the faint glow of the signal fire. Try to think what it would be like and write a short description of what you imagine.

2 Looking towards the shore that winter night you would see only the greyness of sky and hills, the brooding castle and the one welcoming glow of the signal beacon. It is a sight you would remember and it would make an interesting picture. You could paint it like this –

1 Prepare a blue-grey, night sky colour and cover the whole sheet with this paint. Allow it to dry.

2 By adding a little black to your paint make it slightly darker and add the distant hills.

3 Making the paint slightly darker each time now add nearer hills,
– Castle
– Beach and rocks etc.
– Narrow strip of sea at the bottom edge of your paper.
Remember, the nearer it is, the darker it is.

4 Decide where the secret signal fire will be and with a clean brush, clean water and clean paint add the red orange glow of the beacon.

5 Mount the picture and add a caption ready for display.

3 With a map of Scotland, trace Bruce's movements during his campaign to put down those who rebelled against him in Scotland. Try to find out when he was in the various places and make your own map showing this.

4 After the first day of the Battle of Bannockburn it is believed that Robert Bruce may have been thinking about retreat and that only news about the difficult position of the English army caused him to change his mind. Imagine that you are the person who discovered that Edward had marched his soldiers into the marshy ground. How did you find this out? How do you get to see King Robert and tell him? How do you make him believe you? Write the story of your adventure, telling how you helped the Scottish King at Bannockburn.

5 Try to visit King Robert Bruce's memorial at Stirling where you will see models and displays explaining the battle and telling of Bruce's life.

For Freedom Alone

Edward II, safely back in his own court, refused to admit that the Scots were free, and that Bruce was their King, and he went on refusing. For fourteen more years the bloodshed and the burning raged on. All Edward's stubborn efforts to deny the Scots their freedom and to overthrow their King were met by the defiant spears of men with mind and heart set on liberty. Always they refused pitched battle and always they were a ghost army of raiders on nimble horses.

Peace made with the Scots by
Andrew Harclay Earl of Carlisle 1323

An Uneasy Truce

In October 1322, after yet another disastrous campaign in Scotland, Edward II was surprised and almost captured by a Scottish force at Rievaulx Abbey. In the face of defeat and disgrace, he was forced to sign a truce with Scotland in the spring of the following year. He promised also that he would do nothing to prevent the Pope accepting Bruce as the true King of Scots. The peace he kept, his promise he did not. The very next year he sent his Bishop of Winchester to ask the Pope to be even harder on Scotland, to allow only Englishmen to be bishops there. Pope John replied that since no Englishman dare set foot in Scotland then the Church there would have no bishops. He refused the demand.

During the peaceful years of the truce, King Robert showed that he was more than a general whose great ability was known over all Europe. He was a good ruler, humane and just, in days when there was little humanity or justice.

Papal Manoeuvres

But Bruce was faced with many problems. His kingship had not yet been recognised by the Pope, which was hardly surprising. After all, he did come to the throne by way of a dagger stroke on the altar steps of Greyfriars Kirk, and he did crown himself. For many years, the Pope refused to call Robert Bruce by his royal title. Bruce refused to reply unless he was properly addressed. In 1317 when two envoys carrying letters from Pope John did manage to meet the King personally, they were politely received but firmly told that he could not break the seal on letters addressed simply to Robert Bruce since there were several of that name in the kingdom. If the Pope wished him to read something then he must address it properly. King Robert would be glad to help in any way he could. The envoys replied that because of all the problems over Bruce's kingship and the serious complaints made by King Edward II of England, Pope John did not wish to make the case more difficult by calling Bruce 'King' before he

above: Rievaulx Abbey

It was because of King Robert's struggle to be accepted by Pope John that in 1320 a letter was prepared by an assembly of nobles and written in its final form probably by Bernard de Linton who was the Abbot of Arbroath and Chancellor of Scotland. It was a marvellous letter and is known to this day as the Declaration of Arbroath. It was addressed 'To the Most Holy Father in Christ and Lord, the Lord John, by divine providence Supreme Pontiff of the Holy Roman and Universal Church ...'

And was sent by eight earls and thirty-one barons.

The Declaration of Arbroath was a letter to Pope John XXII asking him to tell King Edward of England 'to leave us Scots in peace, who live in this poor little Scotland, beyond which there is no dwelling place at all, and who covet nothing but our own.' If the Pope refused to help, it goes on, then he must accept blame for the 'slaughter of bodies, the perdition of souls and all other misfortunes that follow ...' in both Scotland and England. But it was much more than a cry for help. It was the solemn protest of a small country against the warlike actions of its powerful neighbour. It was the strongest plea for national freedom made during the whole of the fourteenth century on behalf of this or any other country oppressed by nations mightier than themselves and who would fight '... not for glory, nor riches, nor honours ... but for freedom alone.' And it went further. Even though Scotland was a feudal kingdom, its subjects declared a right to rid themselves of their monarch if he did not behave properly, should '... he give up what he had begun, and agree to make us or our kingdom, subject to the King of England or the English ...' Celtic blood flowed in the veins of those who declared this. They remembered the Celtic right to choose their king. It was above all a declaration of man's right to freedom and his duty to defend it. As such it takes its place among the most important documents in the History of the Scottish nation.

had decided if this was proper. Of course Bruce pointed out at once that if calling him 'King' made it more difficult for Edward to win his case, then surely not being called King made it more difficult for Bruce himself. It hardly seemed fair! In parting and more sternly he added that many kings would have given a rougher answer to those who refused to use the royal title. He was thinking perhaps of his old enemy Edward I and his violent temper.

15th century miniature from 'the travels of Sir John Manderville' showing Pope John XXII receiving emissaries

The Declaration of Arbroath

The Declaration begins by telling of Scotland's long history as a free kingdom and how Edward I had taken advantage of its weakness when it had no king and when it was unpractised in war. It then explains that the people have been set free once more by 'our most tireless Prince, King and Lord Robert' to whom all are loyal. But it adds that they will be loyal only for as long as the Lord Robert defends the freedom of the nation. Should he give up what he has begun and agree to make us or our kingdom subject to the King of England or the English, we should exert ourselves at once to drive him out as our enemy . . .' Then in words that have rung down through the centuries it declares: '. . . for, as long as but a hundred of us remain alive we will never in any way be bowed beneath the yoke of English rule. It is not for glory, nor riches, nor honours that we fight, but for freedom alone, that which no man of worth yields up, save with life itself.'

Four Years of Peace

The truce that was agreed between the Scottish King and Edward II after his flight from Rievaulx Abbey, lasted not for the thirteen years planned, but for only four. But it gave Bruce time to organise and repair his war damaged kingdom. Things had changed. Tilling soil and raising crops was always hard enough work, but it seemed hardly worth the effort if the ripe grain was to be harvested by torch and fire so that Edward's men would find no food. Cattle raising was better. Herds and flocks could be driven off and held in safety until the invaders passed. So livestock farming became more and more popular in Scotland. Now there was wool for export to Holland and Germany, as much as five thousand sacks a year; and fleeces and hides too. From this trade came wealth for the kingdom. From the export duty there was wealth for the King. Ships were built to carry these important exports. A navy grew for defence against pirates and to wage war at sea.

The Birth of an Heir

In 1324, the second year of the truce, Robert Bruce's son David was born. He now had a male heir and in his parliament two years later at Cambuskenneth in the shadow of Abbey Craig, the King made final plans for the succession. Those present, which for the first time ever included burgesses and lairds, swore loyalty to the baby prince. They also agreed to pay a ten percent tax to help fill a 'war-emptied' royal treasury.

Cambuskenneth Abbey

England's New King

But the peace did not last. In 1327, Edward II, who had been forced from his throne by a powerful nobility, angry at his failures and excesses, died. He was probably murdered, in a dungeon under Berkeley Castle. On the 1st February Edward III was crowned at Westminster. On the very day of the coronation the Scots attacked and almost seized Norham Castle on the south bank of the River Tweed. But this raid was just a warning. It was not until summer that King Robert, whose patience was now exhausted by English pirate attacks on his shipping, ordered the real advance. In three divisions they rode, crossing the border on 15th June under Douglas, Randolph and Donald of Mar.

Edward III, the boy king, called the great army of England to the royal standard. They gathered at York and marched north on the 10th July, determined to end the raiding and wasting of England's northern counties. At Durham on the 18th July they sighted the Scots' camp fires and marched for two days to close with the 'hobelars' as they were called after the 'hobins' on which they rode. But always the ghost army vanished in the rain and mist. They marched again, north to the River Tyne. There they would cut off the Scots' retreat. They found only seven more days of grey rain and swollen rivers. They turned south again, cold and dispirited, and at last sighted their enemy. The Scots were camped on the south side of the River Wear in a strong position. Randolph and Douglas turned down an invitation from Edward III to come down and fight where he could more easily defeat them. The Scots were very professional soldiers who were not much interested in the rules of chivalry or in being charged by ironclad knights on their mighty horses. It was on the 1st August, that the English army took up its position and two days later the two forces were still looking at each other across the river. That night the Scots vanished again to reappear just as suddenly on the north bank of the Wear at Stanhope. The following night James Douglas boldly led a raiding party deep into the heart of the English positions at Blanchland. The next night, 5th August, the whole Scottish force disappeared once more, this time over the moorland of Stanhope Park and homeward. Edward's great army could not hope to follow. It could only

The tomb of Edward II in Gloucester Cathedral

lumber south to York, dejected and without a battle being fought.

Fighting in Northumberland

No sooner were the Scots raiders safely home than Bruce himself led a fresh army south. The King of Scotland let it be known that he was going to seize the whole of Northumberland and share it out among his loyal followers. This time he attacked the castles with great siege engines, at Norham, Alnwick and Warkworth. He would have no more truces. It would be war or real peace. England's rulers had little choice. Already far too much money, more than £70,000, had been spent on huge armies that had floundered about in the valley of the Wear, hopelessly hunting the nimble raiders on their light horses. There was no money left. England had no option but to accept the terms offered by Robert Bruce. It was never one of the Scottish ambitions that they should rule England, only that they should be left to live in peace in 'this poor little Scotland'. They had fought 'for freedom alone'.

The Treaty of Edinburgh

In the Treaty of Edinburgh, called by some the Treaty of Northampton, Edward declared that Robert Bruce was the King of Scotland and his heirs for all time to come, should have the kingdom without any kind of homage to the King of England. Edward III now admitted that he and other English kings had brought suffering to both realms by claiming to be Lord Superior of Scotland. That claim was now given up and the magnificent 'Prince, the Lord Robert', by grace of God' was King of Scots.

The treaty was sealed at Holyrood in Edinburgh on 17th March 1328, twenty-two years after Robert Bruce had first taken the Crown of Scotland for himself on that fateful Friday in Scone.

Death of Robert Bruce

It was barely a year later at his house in Cardross, where the Leven flows into the widening Clyde, that the soldier King died on the 7th June 1329. He was fifty-five years old. In life, he had led his nation to freedom against impossible odds. In death, though his body was solemnly laid to rest at Dunfermline Abbey, his heart was put in a silver casket, and kept separately by Sir James Douglas, Bruce's mightiest captain. It was while fighting on the Crusade in southern Spain that Douglas, trapped and hopelessly outnumbered by the Moorish cavalry, hurled the casket deep into the enemy ranks and plunged after it crying, 'Douglas will follow thee, or die!' It was later found shielded by his lifeless body and brought back to be buried in Melrose Abbey. Sir James himself was laid to rest in his parish church on the green banks of Douglas Water.

The tomb of Sir James Douglas in St. Bride's Chapel, Douglas

Scotland's Two Kings

A Child King

It was a well ordered nation that Bruce left behind him, free but frail from the wasting effects of war. For the time being the English laid no claim to power in the north, and Scotland once more was a separate kingdom with is own king, who was blessed by the Pope and, for the first time, anointed with holy oil.

But David II was only five years old when he came to the throne. Gone now was the strong hand of his father. Gone too, within three years, were the guardians chosen by Bruce to rule until David was of age. Sir James Douglas died fighting in Spain. Thomas Randolph, Earl of Moray died of a swift and strange illness at Musselburgh. It was too great a chance for the power hungry King of England to miss. More like his grandfather than his father, the warlike Edward III had too a Balliol to thrust upon the Scottish throne, another puppet to dance to an English tune. Only eleven days after Randolph's death Edward Balliol, son of Toom Tabard, sailed north from the River Humber to press his claim with the help of the English King. Five days later he had landed at Kinghorn on the north bank of the wide Firth of Forth and was on the march inland via Dunfermline towards Perth.

Edward Balliol

At daybreak on 11th August 1332, the small invading force not more than one thousand five hundred strong, met the great host of Scots drawn up on the rising moorland north of the River Earn. It should have been an easy enough victory for the Scots at Dupplin Moor but they had forgotten too much of what Bruce had taught. As it was they stood their ground and died there under the rustling clouds of steady arrows from the bowmen of England. Those who escaped the archers pressed forward in confusion and fell before lance, mace and broadsword. In the next month Edward Balliol had himself crowned at Scone and Scotland found herself with two kings.

The coronation of Edward Balliol

Halidon Hill

Though the Scots struck back a week before Christmas sending Balliol scampering south half dressed and on a saddleless horse, he had returned in force the next summer and this time with Edward III in person. On the gentle rise of Halidon Hill outside the walls of Berwick the Scots showed once more that they had not learned from Bruce, not even from Dupplin Moor. Again they fell before the raking volleys from English longbows. Again they were ridden down by the thundering charges of English knights. Now Edward Balliol really was King of Scotland and the child, David II was hurried from his safe keeping at Dumbarton Castle to France where he would find refuge from the English and from the new King of Scots. The land was shared between Balliol and Edward III of England who declared himself Lord Superior of Scotland. All that Robert Bruce had fought for and won throughout his life had been given up within only four short years of his death.

The New Guardians

Another Randolph and another Steward strode forward to lead the fight back. John Randolph was Sir Thomas's son and Robert the Steward was the son of Sir Walter who had commanded a schiltron with James Douglas at Bannockburn. And they drove back the English, almost out of the land, before Sir John Randolph was taken captive in the summer of 1335. Then it was that Sir Andrew Murray, son of Wallace's great friend and fellow commander became Scotland's guardian. For almost three years he carried on the struggle. As Bruce had done before him, Sir Andrew led the English King on a hopeless chase over heatherclad hills and through water-laden marshes.

79

Black Agnes

By August 1337, Sir Andrew Murray was leading raiding parties into the north of England and the plunder seized went some way to pay for Scotland's army. In reply to these and other attacks the English, led by the Earl of Salisbury, laid seige to Dunbar Castle. They came with ships to blockade the port, and engines of war to smash down the stone walls. In the absence of the Earl of March it was his wife who commanded the castle's defence. The Countess, better known as Black Agnes for her tanned skin, was a true sister of Sir John Randolph. She resisted every effort made by the English Earl to break the spirit of the garrison. She strode the battlements taunting the enemy and brushing the dust of war from her rich gown with a handkerchief of silk. For five long months Salisbury hammered on the great walls of Dunbar but without success and had at last to retire having failed to take the castle and perhaps thinking what a poet later put into these words.

'Came I early, came I late
Found I Black Agnes at the gate.'

After three years of bitter conflict Sir Andrew Murray's health failed and he retired to the family castle at Avoch in the Black Isle. He died there in the spring of 1338 having all but freed his country from the power of Edward III. It was Sir John Randolph, now released from captivity, who carried on the struggle. By 1341, Scotland felt strong again, strong enough to take the next step to independence. On 2nd June of that year two ships slipped quietly into the small harbour at Inverbervie, twenty or so miles south of Aberdeen. They had come to the end of their secret passage from France. David, son of Bruce, had come again to his kingdom and with him, his young Queen Joan.

Dunbar castle

David in Scotland

David's reign though long was not glorious. He had returned to a land which had suffered badly from the lean hard years of war. It was at rest now and at last there was time to turn the soil once more and reap a good harvest. For a year or two, David enjoyed himself as any young prince might—jousting and hunting, riding free throughout his kingdom. He also made some effort to repair Scotland's war-damaged government, raising money for the royal treasury and enforcing the law. Parliaments were held at Dundee and Scone. Towns which had been burnt were rebuilt—Haddington, Linlithgow, even Edinburgh, and great abbeys too, like Kelso.

Scone Palace probably stands on the site where the old parliament building stood.

A Mistake

By the autumn of 1346, David found himself with more than one reason or excuse to lead an army against the English. By the terms of a bargain made half a century before between Scotland and France—it was later called the Auld Alliance—each country had a duty to help the other against England. The French king now called upon David to keep his side of the bargain for Edward III had invaded France with a small army and crushed the French at Crécy. Scotland was never too keen to get involved in wars just because of the bargain but this seemed to be an unusually good time. With Edward leading a great army in France, England would be weakened. If David now attacked the northern counties he would be surer of success and perhaps he too could win power and glory there as his mighty father had done. Such an attack would help the French too by forcing Edward to return and defend his kingdom. By the 6th October, the Scottish host had gathered at Perth. They rode south with David at the head, boasting that he would soon see London.

The Battle of Neville's Cross

At first they met with success, but then at first they were attacking only defenceless villages and priories, seizing plunder and demanding payments. By the 16th October David had camped his army outside the city of Durham in Bear Park and it was there he heard that a large English force was approaching from the south. At once the Scots advanced to meet it. Not only did he accept pitched battle which Bruce normally refused, he even turned down Sir John de Grahame's request for some cavalry to scatter the English archers just as the Earl Marshall had done for Bruce at Bannockburn. At Neville's Cross Scotland's army suffered defeat once more because its leaders had forgotten what King Robert had taught. The Scots were routed and David himself found his boast coming true. He soon saw London but not in any way he would have chosen for it was as Edward's prisoner that he entered the city. And he remained a prisoner, though a very comfortable one, for the next eleven years.

Contemporary illumination showing King David II shaking the hand of his captor, Edward III of England, after the battle of Neville's Cross 1346

David arriving at the Tower of London

Balliol Returns

At Neville's Cross Scotland had suffered heavy losses. Her King had been carried off to captivity and Sir John Randolph was dead. Many more of her most powerful nobles had fallen there and it now seemed that England had finally subdued the Scots. King Edward III would soon be Lord Superior of the north. But it was not for another half year that England would move against its northern neighbour. Then Balliol rode out through the gates of Carlisle with a modest army of between three and four thousand to 'recover the realm'. And he was successful. Almost all that had been won from England in the four years before the battle of Neville's Cross was now given up and only the great fortresses at Stirling, Dunbar and Edinburgh still held out. Only this spirited resistance prevented the English occupying all the land up to the ancient Antonine Wall which spans Scotland's narrow waistline, between the Firths of Clyde and Forth.

83

The Black Death

In the years of King David's absence it was Robert the Steward who was again made guardian of the Realm. And they were hard years. The common folk struggled scraping a bare living from scanty crops and small livestock. For a time they watched their enemy in the south suffer dreadfully as the Black Death raged through England. It had come from the East, China perhaps, and crept over Asia and Europe slaughtering fifty million or more. Now it was in Britain and the Scots called it the 'foul death of the English' declaring it to be God's punishment for their sins. They gave thanks to St Andrew for sparing them but they rejoiced too soon. In 1349 the plague's dread shadow spread over the border and for two years the Scottish people died in their thousands, their rotting flesh covered in huge boils and black swellings. The dead were buried in great pits. Most victims died only a few days after the first symptoms appeared—sneezing and red rings on the skin. Survivors lived out each fear-filled day carrying sweet posies against the smell of plague and death.

This was the first visit of the plague and it came to be known as 'the first pestilence'. It returned again and again, the second pestilence in 1362, the third in 1379 and the fourth in 1412. After that the numbers were dropped. No one knows just how many died as a result of that 'first pestilence' but it was the ordinary folk who suffered most. The Black Death was carried by the fleas of rats which infested the thatched roofs of the earthen hovels in which the people lived. Nobles closed their mighty gates against the wretched dying and prayed for their own survival. Fewer fleas in their stone built houses rather than holier living kept the great families alive.

Negotiations for David's Release

King David's gentle captivity in the Tower of London kept him safe from the plague which raged outside its locked doors. Plans for his ransom were made in 1352. Edward offered to return the King of Scots for a modest sum of money and *the right to the Scottish crown if David should be childless*. The English King still earnestly wished to be master of Scotland—but the Scots would have none of it. And they said so with one voice to King David when he was sent by Edward to the Scone Parliament so that he might persuade his subjects to accept the English terms.

Balliol's Resignation

By this time Balliol's position as the other King of Scotland had become hopeless. He had lost even his family home in Buittle near Castle Douglas

and, without support from England, he was powerless. By 1356, Balliol had had enough. At Roxburgh in the January of that year Balliol took the crown from his own head, scooped up a handful of Scottish soil and thrust them both into Edward III's grasping hands. He had resigned his kingship. But more than that, he demanded an ample pension of £2,000 per year for the rest of his life. Balliol had been far too long a penniless king. His retirement would be a wealthy one.

View of Kelso from the remains of Roxburgh castle

Burnt Candlemas

Now it was up to Edward himself to wear the crown of Scotland, if he could. What he was unable to have by peaceful means he would take by conquest. In February, he marched north perhaps hoping to have himself crowned King of Scots at Scone. But his invasion turned out to be a replica of his father's efforts in 1322. Between the Tweed and the Forth nothing had been left of crops or livestock to feed his men. What the Scots themselves had not burned Edward destroyed, setting ablaze the lovely Abbey Church of Haddington called for its beauty 'The Lamp of the Lothians' and plundering the Holy Shrine of Whitekirk a further seven or so miles to the northeast. It was early in February that the burning and wasting took place and since Candlemas Day falls on the second of that month it came to be known as the Burnt Candlemas. Edward reached Edinburgh but the expected supplies did not come. Again the English fleet was the victim of bad weather. The Scots said it had been sent by the Virgin Mary whose shrine the English had spoiled at Whitekirk. Edward's army had to return south and suffer the sudden raids led by another Douglas, the nephew of Sir James, all through their weary trudge to the borders.

King David Returns

But Scotland had suffered so much hardship from plague and war that agreement had to be reached with the English. Robert the Steward as guardian of the Realm arranged for the return of the King on payment of 100,000 marks (almost £67,000) at a rate of 10,000 marks per year. David returned to his kingdom a free man on the 7th October 1357, almost exactly eleven years after he had been taken prisoner at the battle of Neville's Cross. As for the ransom, only three quarters of it was ever paid and even that took twenty years instead of the promised ten.

For the rest of his reign David divided his time between improving the government of his realm and enjoying the luxuries of jousting and hunting, of velvet and silk, paid for with taxes which should have gone towards his ransom. The people forgave him because he was a man of courage and more so, because he was Bruce's son.

His years in captivity had toughened David and he was now master in his own kingdom. Law and order prevailed, business prospered and great nobles were sternly taught not to offend their King. He was planning his third marriage, this time to the daughter of Black Agnes, and dreaming of a child to wear his crown, and of crusades on which holy deeds would be done, when he unexpectedly died at Edinburgh Castle, aged 46, on the 22nd February 1371.

Fashionable dress of the period

The Royal Hunt

Worksection

For Freedom Alone
Understand Your Work

An Uneasy Truce
1 What did Edward II refuse to do when he was safe again in England after his defeat at Bannockburn?
2 What was the result of this?
3 Where was Edward almost captured by the Scots?
4 After this what did he promise King Robert Bruce?
5 Did he keep his promise?
6 What did the Pope say to Edward's request?
7 Who carried Edward's message to the Pope?
8 What kind of ruler was Robert Bruce?

Papal Manoeuvres
1 Why had the Pope not recognised Bruce's kingship?
2 What did Bruce do when the Pope refused to address him as King?
3 How did Bruce reply to the Pope's excuse for not addressing him as King?
4 Was there a kind of threat in his parting words to the Pope's messengers?
5 Why did Robert Bruce refuse the truce offered to him by Edward II after his narrow escape at Rievaulx Abbey?
6 Who was Bernard de Linton?
7 What did Bruce and his nobles do in an attempt to be recognised by the Pope?
8 How many nobles signed the letter?

The Declaration of Arbroath
1 What is the Declaration of Arbroath?
2 What does it say the Pope must do if he refuses the plea?
3 Was it just a cry for help against the English?
4 What does it say the Scots were fighting for?
5 What does it say about loyalty to King Robert?
6 Why was this very surprising?
7 What Celtic right was being remembered here?
8 Even if there were only one hundred Scots left, what would they never do?

Peace and War
1 How long did the truce with Edward II hold?
2 How had farming changed?
3 What could Scotland export now?
4 How did the King get his share of the new wealth?
5 What industry benefited from all this activity?
6 When was the heir to the throne born?
7 Where was Bruce's parliament held?
8 Who were present for the first time in parliament and what did they agree to?

England's New King
1 How did Edward II end his reign?
2 When and how did he die?
3 How did the Scots react to a change of King in England?

4 What caused King Robert to lose patience with the English?
5 How did Edward III attempt to stop the Scottish raids?
6 Was he unsuccessful?
7 How were the Scots able to match an army which was so much stronger?
8 How did the engagement end?

Fighting in Northumberland
1 What did Bruce do when the raiders, led by Randolph, Douglas and Donald of Mar, returned home?
2 Which castles did he attack?
3 Why did the English have to accept Bruce's terms?
4 Why had Bruce done this?
5 What did Edward III agree to by the terms of the Treaty of Edinburgh?
6 When was the treaty sealed?
7 When did King Robert die?
8 What is the story of Bruce's burial and James Douglas' part in it?

Scotland's Two Kings
1 In what state did Robert Bruce leave his kingdom at his death?
2 What age was David II when he came to the throne?
3 What happened to the guardians of the realm chosen by Robert Bruce?
4 What did the King of England do?
5 What happened at Dupplin Moor?
6 What happened within four years of Bruce's death?
7 Who led Scotland's fight back?
8 Who was Black Agnes and what did she do?

David in Scotland
1 Who arrived at Inverbervie on 2nd June 1341?
2 Where had he come from?
3 What state was the kingdom in when he arrived?
4 How did he try to improve his kingdom?
5 Why did he invade England?
6 What happened in the Battle of Neville's Cross?
7 What happened to Scotland after the battle?
8 What castles held out against the English?

The Black Death
1 What was life like in Scotland during the years King David was captive in England?
2 What was the 'foul death of the English'?
3 What struck Scotland in 1349 and when did it return?
4 Who suffered most?
5 How was the Black Death spread?
6 What helped the nobles to survive?
7 In what way was King David's captivity a help to him at this time?
8 What bargain, for the return of their King, did the Scots refuse?

After Balliol

1 Why did Balliol give up his claim to the Scottish throne?
2 When did he resign his crown and how?
3 Did Balliol gain anything from his years as a puppet king?
4 Having failed to regain Scotland by treaty, what did Edward III do now?
5 What happened to his fleet?
6 What did the Scots say caused this to happen?
7 What was this period of waste and war called?
8 What were the terms settled for King David's return to Scotland?
9 Were the terms properly met by the Scots?
10 Why did the people forgive David when he did things which displeased them?
11 Was he a better King when he returned to Scotland in 1357?
12 How long was David's reign?

Use Your Imagination

1 Why do you think it was very unfortunate for the Scots that James Douglas did not manage to capture King Edward II after the Battle of Bannockburn?
2 When Edward II besieged the Scots who had won back Berwick, Bruce did not challenge him in pitched battle. Instead he sent Randolph and Douglas with raiding parties deep into the north of England. Why do you think he did this?
3 Edinburgh is only fifty or so miles from the border while London is more than five times as far. Why do you suppose Bruce found it necessary to keep up an attack on the northern counties of England?
4 When Edward II gathered his strength again in 1322 and marched north against the Scots, Bruce retreated leaving the crops burnt and the cattle byres empty. Why do you think he did this?
5 What mistakes did David II make in his invasion of England?
6 What do you think was the main difference between England's reasons for fighting Scotland, and Scotland's reasons for fighting against England?
7 What conditions caused the Black Death to spread so rapidly?
8 What do you think were the things that people did not understand in the Middle Ages which would have helped them to control the Black Death?
9 When the first astronauts returned from the moon they were kept out of contact with other people for a period. This is called 'quarantine'. Why do you think this is necessary? Can you think of other examples of quarantine?

Further Work

1 Find a copy of the Declaration of Arbroath (translation) and see if you think it was a good letter.

2 It was common for Kings and nobles to go on the Crusades. Find out as much as you can about these 'wars of the cross'. What was the children's crusade?

3 Edward III's fleet was unable to assist the English army at Edinburgh in 1356 because of bad weather. You can paint the kind of seas his sailors would have faced that February. Try it this way:

The Sky
Using very wet paint make a heavy grey sky which looks stormy. Add clouds, torn and jagged by dripping 'cloud colour' on to the wet surface of the background paint. Allow to dry.

Sea Wall
Now cut stone coloured blocks from magazine paper and make a sea wall strong enough to withstand even this storm. Build it stone by stone pasting down each one firmly.

The Storm
Now paint the angry, grey sea with raging waves crashing against the wall. When this is dry use *clean white* paint to add spray, blown by the wind.

4 Imagine you are living in the countryside of Scotland when Edward's army marched north. The Scots retreat burning their crops, driving their livestock into hiding and leaving nothing for the invaders. Describe this when it happens in your village – what you see, hear, think and feel. It could be a letter to a friend telling your story, or a poem.

5 When peace comes again there is a chance for people to live normally, working their farms and doing everyday things. Imagine you are taking a visitor around your village, showing the different things that happened and write an account of the visit.

6 Your friend later takes you on a return visit to the burgh in which he/she lives. What things do you see there? Remember it is your first time in a town. What exciting experiences do you have there?

7 Visit your local museum and see how much you can learn about how ordinary people lived and worked in 14th century Scotland.

The House of the High Steward

Not for a month after David II's death did the Crown of Scotland finally settle on the next royal head. First a flimsy claim to the throne by the Earl of Douglas, the good Sir James' nephew, had to be settled. Only then could Robert the Steward, twice guardian of the realm and for many patient years its heir, be crowned and anointed at Scone on 26th March 1371. So began the royal house of Stewart (the old Scots spelling of Steward) which would rule for three centuries, first in Scotland and then over England too.

King Robert II

This great dynasty began weakly and with little promise. King Robert II was fifty-five years old when he came to the throne. Though he was a grandson of the mighty Bruce he had little of his spirit. He was too gentle to be bold, too tender to be strong. King Robert found it hard enough to control his family, far less rule a kingdom. His third son Alexander was made Earl of Buchan and left to govern the Highlands. Soon enough he was called the Wolf of Badenoch for his brutal ways in the north where he prowled the glens preying on the weak and defenceless. Once in a fit of rage he plundered the city of Elgin, burning and wasting all in sight, even the beautiful cathedral. All this because the Bishop of Moray scolded him for deserting his wife. The Barons that David II had kept down had little respect for their new and weaker King. Soon the kingdom was again at war with England and with itself. The law crumbled and the weak gave way to the strong, honest trade gave way to plunder.

The Auld Alliance and Border Wars

Robert II was no warrior King but still he had to defend his realm against England, and its ambitious kings. The Auld Alliance with France was renewed for the protection it gave and in spite of the warfare it brought. For a time the King managed to keep peace but his nobles were too keen on fighting. The border wars began again led by the Earl of Douglas. He was trying to take back lands occupied by the English but mainly for private reasons, rather than national ones. Douglas reckoned the land was his own. In any case there was plunder to be had and perhaps glory to be won.

The private war was not all on dry land. Scarborough was attacked by sea and the English struck back capturing the fleet of Scottish, French and Spanish ships that had made the pirate raid.

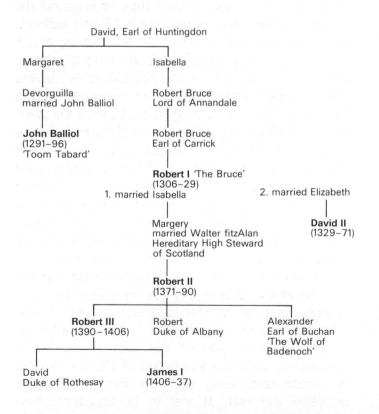

David, Earl of Huntingdon
- Margaret
  - Devorguilla married John Balliol
    - **John Balliol** (1291–96) 'Toom Tabard'
- Isabella
  - Robert Bruce Lord of Annandale
    - Robert Bruce Earl of Carrick
      - **Robert I** 'The Bruce' (1306–29)
        - 1. married Isabella
          - Margery married Walter fitzAlan Hereditary High Steward of Scotland
            - **Robert II** (1371–90)
              - **Robert III** (1390–1406)
                - David Duke of Rothesay
                - **James I** (1406–37)
              - Robert Duke of Albany
              - Alexander Earl of Buchan 'The Wolf of Badenoch'
        - 2. married Elizabeth
          - **David II** (1329–71)

The beginning of the Stewart Line

Walter Fitz Alan was the sixth High Steward of Scotland, a direct descendant of Walter Fitz Alan, son of a Breton knight, who was appointed High Steward by David I in 1136. He was also known as Walter the Steward or Walter Stewart. His son, Robert II, was the first of the Stewart Kings.

Silver coin of Robert II

Preparations for War

The feeble truce between Scotland and England was due to end at Candlemas, the 2nd February 1384. Neither country seemed keen to extend it and in Scotland preparations for war were being made. Castles and strongholds were provisioned and fortified against attack. For the first time a new kind of weapon was brought to Edinburgh—the gun, and stocks of gunpowder were being gathered at other castles. No sooner had the truce ended than the English garrison was driven from Lochmaben Castle and its walls were pulled down. In reply an army from England marched north and held Edinburgh to ransom.

French Support

To encourage the Scots in their war against England and by the terms of the Auld Alliance, the French King sent to King Robert a thousand knights and a great deal of money. The weaker England became through Scottish attack, the better it would be for France. The main party arrived in the May of 1385 but they were not happy allies, the French with the Scots. They had come to fight great battles and win glory in victory and instead found themselves raiding and running in the Scottish way. In time they understood the reasons for this way of fighting but it was difficult for them to watch while the Scots, having struck boldly and deep into England, simply melted away before the advancing English army, laying waste to their own lands as they retreated through Scotland. Richard II pushed north with his great army, and in revenge for the raids burned abbeys and towns alike, even Edinburgh. The French leader, Admiral Jean de Vienne, understood better when he saw Richard swing south again with a starving army to run the gauntlet of constant raiding and ambushing of his weary troops. And he understood better still when the Scots cleared out the English from Roxburgh where they had been since Edward Balliol's time.

After a year or two of uneasy truces the Scots struck again, alone this time and on two fronts. The larger force lead by the Earl of Fife swept down the west side of the country as far as Stainmore, 20 miles south-east of Penrith, while, to create confusion, the new Earl of Douglas attacked the east. It was to be this force that would win the greater fame.

Chevy Chase

Douglas plundered freely right to the walls of Newcastle before turning north again carrying, in triumph, the captured standard of Henry Percy, Earl of Northumberland—called Hotspur for his fiery temper. Percy chased the Scots and his standard with all possible speed and closed on the raiders at Otterburn near Hadrian's Wall, by the failing light of a low August sun. Furious battle was joined almost at once and all through that night the close combat raged. Deadly English arrows lay useless in their quivers so tightly mixed were the forces. Sword and dagger, lance and battle-axe stabbed and hacked in a wild fury of shining steel and blood, sharply lit by the clean, cold light of a bright summer moon. By unknown hands Douglas fell mortally wounded. He told those who carried him to the rear that they should keep his death secret and return to the fight carrying his banner and carrying out his battle cry— 'A Douglas! A Douglas!' Though heavily outnumbered, the day was won by the Scots and Henry Percy was made captive. A dead man had won the field. The Battle of Otterburn, or Chevy Chase as it is sometimes called, was not really important, except perhaps to Sir John Montgomery of Eaglesham and Eglinton who took a huge ransom for the return of proud Hotspur. It is so well remembered because of the fine poetry it inspired in the noble Ballad of Otterburn, where Douglas is made to say:

'But I hae dreamed a dreary
    dream
Beyond the Isle of Skye;
I saw a dead man win a fight
And I think that man was I.

My wound is deep, I fain
    would sleep
Take thou the vanguard of me
And hide me by the bracken
    bush
That grows on yonder lily
    lee.'

Memorial of the Battle of Otterburn

Otterburn Battle site?

King Robert III

The troubles went on under King Robert II and more so under his son John, an even milder spirit, who came to the throne in 1390. He took the name Robert because there had been so many ill-fated 'Johns'. But fate was not to be cheated so easily and Robert III's reign was a bleak time for Scotland.

In the Highlands too, clans struggled and fought for power and land. To settle one particular feud between the clans Chatton and Kay a duel was arranged between thirty chosen warriors from each side. This amazing contest took place on 28th September 1396, on the North Inch of Perth. A special ring was prepared for the mortal combat and King Robert III acted as a kind of royal referee. Only a handful survived and even they were badly wounded. And it settled nothing, of course.

Too often King Robert III acted as a kind of royal referee, an onlooker as his kingdom tore itself apart in bitter conflict among powerful nobles jealous of one another's power.

A Misadventure

Prince James became heir to the throne when his elder brother David died, possibly having been murdered whilst in the care of their uncle. Now he alone stood between that uncle and the crown of Scotland. The ailing king no longer felt strong enough to keep his young prince safe and in 1406, when James was twelve, new plans were made for his security. At Leith on the 14th March, a Polish merchant ship, the Maryenknyght, left harbour bound for France with a cargo of hides and wool. It carried also Prince James. In France, he would find safety from his uncle's royal ambitions. A few days later the ship was seized by English pirates off Flamborough Head twenty miles south of Scarborough. Though there was a truce between Scotland and England, at the time neither the English pirates nor the English King thought it reason enough to give up such prize as the Prince of Scotland. James was imprisoned in the Tower. King Robert now very feeble, heard the news on the Isle of Bute. The grief it brought him ended his life. He died on 4th April 1406, Palm Sunday of that year.

In his own life King Robert III had been a mild and gentle person always too much aware of

The tomb of Robert III in Paisley Abbey

his own failings, always judging himself over harshly. For his epitaph he chose the words— 'Here lies the worst of Kings and the most wretched of men in the whole realm.' For his place of burial he suggested a deep midden. He was laid to rest not in such a place but in Paisley Abbey which his ancestors had founded two and a half centuries before, and where his father had been born.

Worksection

The House of the High Steward
Understand Your Work

King Robert II
1 Of what royal house was Robert II the first King?
2 Where and when was he crowned?
3 How long did this royal house last?
4 Where did it rule?
5 Was Robert II a strong King?
6 Who was the Wolf of Badenoch?
7 How did he earn his name?
8 What caused him to plunder Elgin?

The Auld Alliance and War
1 Why did King Robert renew the Auld Alliance with France?
2 What was the Earl of Douglas doing in the border country and why?
3 Where else was the raiding going on?
4 As the end of the truce with England approached, Scotland was making certain preparations. What were these?
5 What new weapon was now being developed?
6 What happened when the truce ended?
7 How did England reply?

French Support
1 What aid did the French King give the Scots?
2 In what way did this help the French themselves?
3 Why did the French knights dislike fighting alongside the Scots?
4 How did the French learn to understand the fighting methods of the Scots?
5 What led to the Battle of Chevy Chase?
6 Why were the English archers unable to use their bows in the battle?
7 When their leader Douglas was killed what did the Scots do?
8 How was it that a dead man won this battle?

King Robert III
1 Why did Robert II's son call himself King Robert III instead of John?
2 Was he a successful King?
3 What was the amazing event which took place on 28th September 1396, on the North Inch of Perth?
4 What part did King Robert III play in this affair?
5 What was the result?
6 Why was King Robert III fearful for the safety of Prince James?
7 What did he do about this?
8 Was the King's plan for James' safety successful?
9 How long did the King live after he heard the outcome of his plan?

10 What was Robert III's opinion of himself as a King and as a man?
11 Where is he buried?

Use Your Imagination
1 Why do you suppose it was very important to have a strong king in the Middle Ages?
2 Do you think it was necessary for the king to be more than simply strong? What other qualities should he have?
3 What is meant by a 'private war'?
4 Do you think guns would make any difference to the design of castles?
5 Why do you think the Scots retreated further and further north as the English army advanced? Why not keep out of sight?
6 How does it help an invader to strike at two places rather than one?
7 Can you imagine why the name Hotspur was chosen to mean 'fiery tempered'?
8 What do you think is meant by saying that Robert III acted too often like a 'royal referee'?
9 Why did knights in battle show their coats-of-arms on their shields and surcoats?
10 Can you think of any reasons why all the knights on one side did not wear one colour and all their opponents another colour, like football teams?

Further Work
1 With nine different colours, nine knights in armour could be recognised by their colour. But there were more than nine knights! If they were allowed two colours per knight, does this help? How many different pairs can you make? Try this –

   1 Draw a row of eight shields, like this one

   2 Choose nine different colours – say, red, yellow, blue, green, purple, orange, black, white, brown
   3 Colour the left half of each shield in the *same* colour.
   4 Now colour the other half of each shield with a *different* one of your eight remaining colours
   5 When your eight shields are ready choose another colour from your nine for the left half and make a row of eight more shields, all different

How many shields can you make altogether? How many knights can now be recognised?

How could you make even more patterns for different knights still using the same nine colours, two per shield?

2 See if you can find a copy of the Ballad of Otterburn to read and enjoy.

3 Here is a way you can make a picture of two knights jousting:

Take some black scrap paper and cut it into rough shapes for the head, neck, body, tail and legs of a horse. Now use these to help you paint a galloping horse. First, arrange the head, neck and body. Then cut the legs in two parts so that they can 'bend' and arrange them in a galloping stride. (Do the back legs bend the same way as the front?) Finally add the flowing tail.

When you are satisfied that your horse is going at full tilt, use it as a model to help you paint a picture of two horses galloping towards each other.

When the paint is dry, add the knights in full armour emblazoned with colourful coats-of-arms and with their lances levelled. (Remember the flowing trappers for your horses.)

You can add a background of tents, stands, people watching, flags waving and also the rails, *on each side* of which the knights are riding.

shields to decorate the rails

4 Are there still knights today? Do they have coats-of-arms? Who is the Lord Lyon? Find out what you can about heraldry today?

5 A cavalry charge of fully armoured knights was a frightening sight for foot soldiers in their schiltrons. Write a list of words which describe the sight, sound, feelings from the point of view of the foot-soldier. Try to arrange your list as a kind of poem.
Each verse could begin 'Nearer and nearer, Louder and louder', and end with 'Now comes the charge'.

Like this –
Nearer and nearer
Louder and louder
Thunder of hooves
Clanking of steel
Now comes the charge

Nearer and nearer
Louder and louder
....
....
Now comes the charge
And so on . . .

If you like you could rewrite your finished poem starting with very small writing in the first verse and getting bigger and bigger verse by verse – just like the knights as they came closer . . .

6 Try to arrange a visit to Paisley Abbey where you will learn more about the Stewarts

Acknowledgements

Moffat: Scottish History, Book 2
The Publisher would like to thank the following for permission to reproduce photographs:

Aerofilms Ltd., p. 20, p. 25, p. 46; All Sport/Photographic Ltd., p. 22 (top); Ashmolean Museum, p. 8, p. 90; John Brennan, p. 36, p. 44, p. 55, p. 61, p. 72, p. 75, p. 80, p. 81, p. 85, p. 92; British Library, p. 13, p. 56 (bottom), p. 73, p. 82; Duke of Buccleuch (Scottish Record Office), p. 22 (bottom); Courtauld Institute of Art, p. 76; Dean and Chapter of Westminster, p. 39 (top), p. 61; Ann Dean, p. 62; Department of the Environment, Edinburgh, p. 77 (bottom); C. M. Dixon, p. 32; Professor G. Donaldson (Scottish Record Office), p. 49; Dennis Hardley Photography, p. 63; H.M.S.O. (A. G. Ingram Ltd.), p. 74; Kyle and Carrick District Council (J. Stewart McLauchlan), p. 9; Frank Martin Photography, p. 93; Studio Morgan, Aberdeen, p. 43; Sir David Ogilvy (National Library of Scotland), p. 52; Perth High Street Excavation Committee, p. 24; Public Record Office, p. 37, p. 39 (bottom), p. 56, p. 72; Roxburghe Estates (National Library of Scotland), p. 4; Scottish Record Office, p. 77; Dr Duncan Thomson, p. 64.

Back cover photo: Frank Martin Photography

Illustrations by Robert Ayton, Norma Burgin, Stephen Cocking, Dan Escott, Oliver Frey, Richard Hook, John James, Chris Molan, Tony Morris, David Palmer, Graham Smith and Michael Whittlesea.